English for Academic Study

New edition

Vocabulary

Study Book

Colin Campbell

ISLC
International Study and Language Centre

University of Reading

Garnet EDUCATION

Credits

Published by

Garnet Publishing Ltd
8 Southern Court
South Street
Reading RG1 4QS, UK

This edition first published 2012.

ISBN: 978 1 90861 443 8

British Cataloguing-in-Publication Data. A catalogue record for this book is available from the British Library.

Every effort has been made to trace the copyright holders and we apologize in advance for any unintentional omission. We will be happy to insert the appropriate acknowledgements in any subsequent editions.

Production

Project manager:	Fiona Dempsey
Project consultant:	Fiona McGarry
Editorial team:	Lucy Constable, Fiona Dempsey, Mara Rizzi, Sarah Whiting
Art director:	Mike Hinks
Design and layout:	Simon Ellway, Maddy Lane, Ian Lansley
Photography:	Alamy, Clipart.com, Corbis, Getty, iStock

Printed and bound in Lebanon by International Press: interpress@int-press.com

The author and publisher wish to acknowledge the following use of material:

Atkinson, R. L., Atkinson, R. C., Smith, E. E., Bem, D. J., & Nolen-Hoeksema, S. (1999). *Hilgard's Introduction to Psychology*. California, CA: Wadsworth Pub Co.

Ehrenberg, R.G., Brewer, D. J., Gamoran, A., & Willms, J.D. (2001, November). Does class size matter? *Scientific American*, *285*(5), 78–85

Fulcher, J. & Scott, J. (1999) *Sociology*. Oxford: Oxford University Press.

Rowntree, D. (1981). *Statistics without Tears: A Primer for Non-Mathematicians*. London: Penguin.

Staff. (2001, May 10). *On the move. The Economist*. Retrieved from http://www.economist.com.

Understanding Global Issues. (1998). *The Global Village: Challenges for a Shrinking Planet* [Pamphlet]. Buckley, R.

Zorpette, G. (2001, November). The Asian Paradox [Sidebar]. *Scientific American*, *285*(5), 84.

Acknowledgements

I would like to thank all the teachers and students at the ISLC and in other institutions who have given feedback and pointed out mistakes in earlier versions of this book, which has allowed us to offer this updated version.

Colin Campbell, March 2012

Contents

Book map

	Unit	Skills focus
1	**Multi-meaning words**	■ Choosing meaning from context ■ Different word class, different meaning ■ Review
2	**Word classes – nouns, verbs, adjectives and adverbs**	■ Identifying word classes in context ■ Words belonging to one class only ■ Words belonging to two or more classes ■ Review
3	**Word families and word parts**	■ Words that do not change form ■ Understanding word families through suffixes ■ Understanding meaning through prefixes ■ Negative prefixes ■ Family members that look different from each other ■ Complete word families ■ Cohesion: Using nouns and verbs to connect ideas ■ Word parts ■ Review
4	**Collocations**	■ Learning from texts ■ Using a dictionary to learn collocations ■ Verb + noun combinations ■ Verb + noun + preposition combinations ■ Adjective + noun combinations ■ Adverb + verb, adverb + adjective combinations ■ Review
5	**Word grammar**	■ Combining nouns ■ 'Noun followed by noun' complement clauses ■ Other noun patterns ■ Noun + noun combinations ■ Adjectives and what follows them ■ Verbs and verb patterns ■ Transitive and intransitive verbs ■ Verbs followed by *that* + clause ■ Verbs followed by *wh~* words ■ Review
6–10	**AWL – Sublists 1–5**	■ Meanings of words ■ Multi-meaning words ■ Word classes ■ Word families ■ Collocations ■ Word grammar ■ Review

i Introduction

Aims of the course

This book has been designed with several aims in mind: to clarify what you need to know in order to use words correctly; to introduce over 450 key **word families** and to provide you with extensive practice in their use; to clarify the type of information that dictionaries can give you on how to use words appropriately and effectively; and to provide you with practice in the use of dictionaries.

Although this book is intended for self-study outside formal classes, you should discuss with your teacher any problems you face in using the book. You will find this useful if you do not understand some of the **terminology**, or if your answers do not match the ones in the answer key.

Structure of the course

- **Part 1:** These five units, 1–5, provide you with an introduction to vocabulary development, based on words from the **General Service List** (see below). Each unit focuses on one aspect of the effective learning of vocabulary. For example, Unit 2 looks at **word classes**, i.e., the different grammatical classes that words belong to: nouns, verbs, etc. Unit 5 looks at **word grammar**, i.e., how individual words are used in sentences and how they connect with other words, or with other parts of the sentence.
- **Part 2:** These five units, 6–10, provide practice in using key academic words, building on the practice in Units 1–5. Each unit practises the five aspects of vocabulary learning that were covered in Part 1, starting with **multi-meaning words** and ending with word grammar.
- **Study tips:** These have been included for ease of reference when you are revising what you have studied. They either summarize the outcome of a series of activities or are a summary of other information contained in the unit.

Additional materials

Glossary: Words or phrases in **bold** (or **bold** and <u>underlined</u> in task instructions) in the text are explained in the glossary on pages 165–166.

Answer key: Answers for all the exercises are provided.

Academic Word List: All the academic words dealt with in Units 6–10 are provided in a word list.

Achievement test: This tests how much progress you have made in your understanding of words and your knowledge of how words work. You can either do this test when you have done all the exercises in the book, or you can do the test twice: once before you start doing the exercises in this book, and the second time after you have done all the exercises.

The vocabulary in the book

- **General Service List (GSL):** This contains over 2,000 word families that are frequently used in a wide variety of contexts. These are words you will use in both general and academic texts. You may already be familiar with many of these words, but there are many you will be less familiar with or not know at all. In addition, you may not have all the information you need in order to use even the familiar words correctly and with confidence. In Units 1–5, you will practise words from about 150 of the most important GSL word families.
- **Academic Word List (AWL):** This word list contains word families based on words that occur frequently in different academic subjects. They are words that you will need when speaking and writing during your course of academic study. These are not technical words, but ones that you will meet in texts, regardless of the subjects you study.

The full AWL is divided into ten sublists. The first nine lists contain 60 word families each and the last list contains 30 word families. In this book, we introduce word families from the first five sublists. Unit 6 introduces words from AWL Sublist 1; Unit 7 introduces word families from AWL Sublist 2, and so on. In total, you will practise words from 300 word families from the AWL. For information on the development and evaluation of the AWL, see Coxhead, A.(2000). A New Academic Word List, *TESOL Quarterly*, *34* (2), 213–238.

You can find the full list on the Internet by entering 'Academic Word List' in any search engine.

■ **Technical words:** In addition to learning words from the General Service List and the Academic Word List, you will also need to learn many technical words connected with your own subject. These words represent concepts that are perhaps only found in your subject area.

There are a number of ways of learning these words. You can:
- read articles or books connected with your subject
- listen to lectures or watch programmes connected with your subject
- find an Internet glossary on your subject

In all of the above cases, you should make a record of commonly occurring words and study how they are used. Remember, however, that with some technical words you may not fully understand what they mean until you have been on your academic course for some time.

How to use this book

In order to help you use this book effectively, we have included some recommendations on how to work through the units.

It is recommended that you work through the units in this book in the order they appear. It is also recommended that you do the exercises in the order they appear within the units and also that you do all the exercises. Many words are recycled throughout the exercises; in other words, they appear a number of times in different exercises. Doing all the exercises will give you more practice in recognizing and using the words.

■ At the end of each unit, there is an activity which encourages you to review all the exercises you have done in the unit, and to write down new phrases or new words that you have learnt. Reviewing vocabulary, i.e., looking again and again at words you have met, is an essential part of learning vocabulary. It is not enough to see words once in order to remember them; if you only meet a word once, you will not have all the information you need to use it fully and correctly.

■ It is also useful to record whole **phrases** or sentences with new words in them rather than just the words by themselves, as this will help you to be able to use the words when speaking or writing.

■ For some exercises the instructions tell you to use a dictionary, but even in cases where there is no explicit instruction to do so, a good **monolingual dictionary** will be of great help to you. It is important to stress that a good monolingual dictionary will not only be useful in doing the exercises in this book, but will also help you during your continuing language studies.

■ You should check your answers when you finish each exercise. If you have made a mistake, notice the correct answer and go back and look at the exercise again. If you still cannot understand why this is the correct answer, ask one of your teachers.

■ It is important that you review the words you learn in a regular and systematic way, for example, by reviewing words at the end of each day, then again at the end of each week and again after two weeks.

Part 1: Introduction to Vocabulary Development

In these units you will be studying five aspects of effective vocabulary study based on words from the General Service List.

Each unit will address one aspect, as follows:

- **Unit 1:** Multi-meaning words
- **Unit 2:** Word classes – nouns, verbs, adjectives and adverbs
- **Unit 3:** Word families and word parts
- **Unit 4:** Collocations
- **Unit 5:** Word grammar

These five aspects of vocabulary learning will then be used in Part 2 to help you study the frequent word families that are listed in the Academic Word List Sublists 1–5.

Multi-meaning words

In this unit you will:

- learn the different meanings of common words with more than one meaning
- understand the function of different word classes

Introduction

One of the problems with using dictionaries to find the meaning of words is that many words have a number of different meanings. If you select the first meaning you find in the dictionary without thinking about the context in which the word appears, you may choose the wrong definition and misunderstand the text.

Here are some examples of common words with very different meanings:

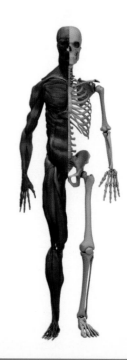

Word	Meaning
body	<ul><li>the physical structure of a person or animal, including the head and limbs</li><li>a group of people who are connected through their work or a particular purpose, e.g., *The WHO is an international body concerned with health issues.*</li><li>a large amount of something, especially something that has been collected, such as knowledge, information and so on, e.g., *There is now a considerable body of evidence to support the theory that life exists in other solar systems.*</li></ul>
capital	<ul><li>the city where a country has its main seat of government</li><li>money or property used to start a business</li></ul>

Task 1   Choosing meaning from context

Many words can only be fully understood in context. This is particularly true for **homonyms**, i.e., words that have two or more unrelated meanings. The following exercises provide the context of single sentences. When reading at the paragraph level, however, you should also use context beyond the sentence level.

1.1   **Choose the correct meaning of the underlined words according to the context in which they appear.**

1. The government gets a lot of revenue from <u>duty</u> on tobacco products.
   a. a moral or legal obligation
   b. a task you have to do as part of your job
   c. a tax you pay on goods you buy

2. The questions in the booklet can be answered in any <u>order</u>.
   a. the arrangement or sequence of a group of things in relation to each other
   b. a command given by a person in authority
   c. a request for a product to be delivered to you

3. Universities are considering making work experience skills <u>count</u> towards a degree.
   a. to calculate the quantity of things or people there are in a group
   b. to be valuable or important
   c. to say numbers in order

4. The <u>nature</u> of the task demands a person with a lot of experience in engineering.
   a. a combination of qualities or features that define a thing
   b. the physical world, including all living things and features such as the land, the oceans and the weather
   c. the character of a person or animal

5. Fatigue is one of the most <u>common</u> causes of road accidents.
   a. frequent
   b. belonging to or used by a group of people
   c. ordinary or usual

6. The whole <u>point</u> of the new law is to protect the rights of individuals.
   a. an idea or opinion that forms part of an argument or discussion
   b. the aim of or reason for something
   c. a precise moment in time or in the development of something

7. Investing in Amazon should provide an excellent <u>return</u>.
   a. go back to one place from another place
   b. profit on money invested
   c. restarting an activity after not doing it for some time

8. Police arrested 15 people in a security <u>operation</u> in the capital.
   a. the process of cutting into a human body for medical purposes
   b. a business, company or organization
   c. a planned action for a particular purpose

9. There are still numerous one-party <u>states</u> around the world.
   a. the condition of a person or thing at a particular time
   b. a country or nation
   c. an area within a country that has its own legal and political powers

10. Young people today have a greater <u>degree</u> of independence than 50 years ago.
    a. an amount of something
    b. a unit for measuring the size of an angle
    c. a recognition awarded by a university

11. The government plans to <u>introduce</u> a system of identity cards.
    a. to bring a plan, product or system into operation for the first time
    b. to tell an audience about a performance or speaker they are going to see or hear
    c. to formally tell people each other's names when they meet for the first time

1.2 **Here are ten more words to guess in context. Choose the correct meaning, as in Ex 1.1.**

1. The new mayor has radical <u>views</u> about the best way to deal with the increase in violent crime.
   a. opinions or beliefs about something
   b. what you are able to see from a particular place
   c. a picture or photograph of a place

2. The <u>terms</u> of the contract must be acceptable to both sides.
   a. a word or expression used to refer to something
   b. the conditions of an agreement
   c. one of the periods of time that the school or university year is divided into

3. It is difficult to disagree with the <u>argument</u> that oil has been the main reason for a number of recent military conflicts.
   a. a dispute between two or more people, usually angry
   b. a set of reasons offered as proof that your opinion is right

4. It is quite <u>certain</u> that the continued rise in the temperature of the oceans will lead to catastrophe sooner or later.
   a. confident that something is true
   b. sure to happen
   c. used to talk about a particular person or thing without naming them or describing them exactly

5. There are no simple <u>solutions</u> to the problem of global warming.
   a. a way of solving a problem
   b. the correct answer to a problem in mathematics or a puzzle of some kind
   c. a liquid in which a solid or gas has been dissolved

6. A large <u>number</u> of conditions can be treated with this drug.
   a. a word or sign that represents a quantity or an amount
   b. a quantity of, e.g., things or people
   c. a single item in a performance, e.g., a piece of music

7. Nature, in the broadest <u>sense</u>, is equivalent to the natural world, physical world, or material world.
   a. one of the five natural abilities – sight, hearing, feeling, taste and smell
   b. a feeling based on instinct rather than fact
   c. the meaning of a word, phrase or sentence

8. The regulations have been introduced in order to safeguard the <u>interests</u> of local people.
   a. activities or subjects you enjoy in your spare time
   b. an advantage that benefits a particular cause
   c. amount, usually a percentage, paid for the use of someone's money

9. There is a strong <u>case</u> for increasing tax on luxury items.
   a. an example of something happening
   b. a set of reasons why something should happen or be done
   c. a legal matter that will be dealt with in court

10. Elderly patients are often in a bad <u>way</u> following medical operations.
    a. a method of doing something
    b. condition
    c. a route you take to go somewhere

| Task 2 | Different word class, different meaning |

Words can sometimes belong in different classes. For example, *mean* can be a noun, adjective or verb. Some of these words can have a different meaning depending on the **word class.**

Word	Meaning
mean (noun)	an average
mean (verb)	to have a particular meaning
mean (adjective)	unwilling to spend money

2.1 **Choose the correct word class for the underlined words. Then check your answer by looking at the definitions.**

1. The article <u>addresses</u> the issue of overfishing in the North Sea.
    a. noun: where someone lives
    (b) verb: to begin trying to solve a problem

2. Experts believe the current instability in world stock markets will not <u>last</u> long.
    a. adjective: coming after all the others
    b. verb: continue or endure for a particular length of time

3. The company director is a powerful leader and people rarely <u>question</u> his decisions.
    a. noun: a phrase you ask when you want information
    b. verb: to express doubts about something

4. The <u>key</u> issue in the next election will almost certainly be the economy.
    a. adjective: most important
    b. noun: a metal instrument used for opening or locking a door

5. Many analysts believe the country is entering a period of <u>relative</u> economic instability.
    a. noun: a family member
    b. adjective: having a particular quality in comparison with something else

6. The company intends to <u>form</u> an alliance with a partner company in China.
    a. verb: to bring into existence
    b. noun: a particular type of something

7. The final decision on the company's merger is usually made by the <u>board</u>.
    a. verb: to get on a plane, train, ship, etc.
    b. noun: a group of people who manage a company

8. Environmentalists <u>object</u> to the proposed new motorway.
    a. verb: to express disapproval or opposition to something
    b. noun: a physical thing that you can see, hold or touch

9. It is a <u>matter</u> of concern that security at some airports is not up to international standards.
    a. noun: a topic that you discuss, think about or deal with
    b. verb: to be important

10. Unilever is known for its <u>sound</u> financial management.
    a. noun: something that you hear
    b. adjective: well-founded, sensible, trustworthy

2.2 **Use your dictionary to check the meanings of the underlined words in the text below. Write the appropriate definition for the words as they appear in the text.**

Study tip

Whenever possible, use a comprehensive dictionary which provides example sentences.

Education is a pillar of modern <u>society</u> and the <u>subject</u> of endless, often passionate, arguments about how it can best be improved. In the US, there is <u>heated</u> debate following revelations that the country's secondary school students <u>perform</u> poorly relative to many Asian and European students. The news coincided with increasing <u>concern</u> over the nation's urban and lower-income suburban schools, too many of which are languishing at achievement levels <u>far</u> below those of middle-class and upper middle-class suburban schools.

Source: Ehrenberg, R. G., Brewer, D. J., Gamoran, A., & Willms, J. D. (2001, November). Does class size matter? *Scientific American, 285*(5), 78–85.

1. society

   people living together in organized groups, with rules and traditions governing the way they behave towards one another

2. subject

   _____

   _____

3. heated

   _____

   _____

4. perform

   _____

   _____

5. concern

   _____

   _____

6. far

   _____

   _____

Task 3   Review

3.1   **Each of these words from Unit 1 can belong to more than one word class. Write all the word classes that each word belongs to in the spaces provided.**

1. key   _adjective_   _verb_   _noun_   _____

2. subject   _____   _____   _____   _____

3. relative   _____   _____   _____   _____

4. form   _____   _____   _____   _____

5. sound   _____   _____   _____   _____

6. order   _____   _____   _____   _____

7. object   _____   _____   _____   _____

8. matter   _____   _____   _____   _____

9. question   _____   _____   _____   _____

3.2   **Choose four of the words in Ex 3.1 and write them in sentences to show their meaning.**

> **Study tip**
>
> You may need to write down and use a word several times before you remember it.

1. _object_ _____

    I object to the way many people treat their pets.

    In the past, women were treated as objects.

2. _____

    _____

    _____

3. _____

    _____

    _____

4. _____

    _____

    _____

5. _____

    _____

    _____

3.3 **Look again at the tasks in this unit and write down any new words or phrases you have learnt.**

Make sure you record which word class or word classes the words belong to.

Note: You will learn more about word classes in Unit 2.

Make your own notes here.

duty (noun) – e.g., customs duty on luxury cars

For web resources relevant to this book, see:
www.englishforacademicstudy.com

These weblinks will give you access to an online dictionary with clear, uncomplicated **entries**, sites containing explanations of words with multiple meanings, and exercises and activities that allow you to test yourself.

2 Word classes – nouns, verbs, adjectives and adverbs

In this unit you will:

- identify the four main word classes from context
- expand your vocabulary
- develop your reading skills at sentence level

Introduction

Knowing the word class for an individual word will help you use it correctly in both writing and speaking. The main classes we will look at in this unit are nouns, verbs, adjectives and adverbs.

> Educators have a multitude of explanations for why smaller class sizes might be expected to improve academic performance, although frequently the ideas are anecdotal.

Source: Ehrenberg, R. G., Brewer, D. J., Gamoran, A., & Willms, J. D. (2001, November). Does class size matter? *Scientific American, 285*(5), 78–85.

Here are some examples of word classes from the text above:

Nouns	educators, multitude, explanations, class, sizes, performance
Verbs	have, might, expect, improve, are
Adjectives	smaller, academic, anecdotal
Adverbs	frequently

Note: Sometimes you can only identify word class from context.

Example:

- *He studies hard for his exams. (v)*
- *They work hard in their studies. (n)*

Study tip

When you find a word you have recently learnt in an academic text, use the context to make sure you are clear about its meaning.

Task 1   Identifying word classes in context

1.1   **Read the text and complete the table below. Put the underlined words in the correct column according to their word class.**

Study after study ranks schoolchildren in Japan and other developed Asian countries among the best in the world, particularly on standardized tests of Mathematics and Science. American high school students, meanwhile, have slipped somewhere below those in Greece, Lithuania, Taiwan and Singapore in advanced Mathematics and Science. However, classes in Asia are large; forty students for one teacher would be normal in most of the region. In contrast, elementary school class sizes in the United States average about 24, according to the US Department of Education.

Source: Zorpette, G. (2001, November). The Asian Paradox [Sidebar]. *Scientific American, 285*(5), 84.

Nouns	Verbs	Adjectives	Adverbs

Task 2   Words belonging to one class only

2.1   **Use your dictionary to check these words and write which word class they belong to.**

Word	Word class	Word	Word class
growth	noun	regular	
entire		relatively	
basically		provide	
avoid		prevent	
existence		highly	
discover		security	

Note: The following common patterns will help in identifying word class. Words ending in:

- ~th, ~ence, ~ity are usually nouns
- ~ly are usually adverbs

> **Study tip**
>
> Allocate time on a weekly basis to review new words you have been learning.

2.2 **Decide what word class would fill each gap in these sentences. Write _v_ (verb), _n_ (noun), _adj_ (adjective) or _adv_ (adverb) in the brackets after each gap.**

1. Researchers have _____ (_v_) that some computer users are spending up to 15 hours a day at their machines.

> **Study tip**
>
> It can be useful to link new words with any related **synonyms** and **antonyms** that you know. For example, _growth_: synonym – _increase_, antonym – _decrease_.

2. E-commerce is a _____ (__) recent phenomenon.

3. A virus could potentially destroy the _____ (__) database.

4. Online _____ (__) is becoming an increasing problem in e-commerce.

5. We've seen an enormous _____ (__) in the number of businesses that operate solely through the Internet.

6. The installation of anti-spam software can _____ (__) unwanted e-mails reaching your computer.

7. The new network system is _____ (__) sound.

8. There are simple measures that can be taken to _____ (__) becoming a victim of computer fraud.

9. The _____ (__) of organized criminal gangs targeting the Internet is not in doubt.

10. Criminals have developed _____ (__) sophisticated techniques to bypass computer security systems.

11. Most experts recommend _____ (__) security checks.

12. All universities should _____ (__) more computer facilities for students.

2.3 **Complete the sentences in Ex 2.2 with words from Ex 2.1. In the case of verbs, pay attention to the ending required, e.g., ~s, ~ed, ~ing, etc.**

Example: Researchers have _discovered_ (v) that some computer users are spending up to 15 hours a day at their machines.

Task 3	Words belonging to two or more classes

We noted in Task 1 that some words can belong to more than one word class.

Example:
The word _average_ can be a noun, a verb or an adjective.

- _In the years between 1982 and 1988, the economy grew at an **average** of nearly 3 per cent per year. (n)_
- _Inflation **averaged** just under 2.8 per cent per year. (v)_
- _The **average** cost of making a movie has risen by 15 per cent. (adj)_

3.1 Use a dictionary to check the different word classes these words belong to.

Word	Word class
excess	noun, adjective
stem	
match	
influence	
lack	

Word	Word class
spare	
joint	
risk	
sample	
rank	

3.2 The words from the table in Ex 3.1 appear in the following sentences. Write *n, v, adj* or *adv* to show which word class they belong to.

1. A decline in soft drinks sales has left the industry with <u>spare</u> capacity. (adj)
2. Many factories saw <u>excess</u> production during the first six months of the year. (___)
3. However, <u>lack</u> of investment has been the major problem for many companies in the drinks sector. (___)
4. Britvic's performance has not <u>matched</u> that of its competitors. (___)
5. Pepsi-Cola <u>ranks</u> as one of the world's biggest manufacturers. (___)
6. Many companies have entered into <u>joint</u> venture agreements with Eastern European companies. (___)
7. Drinks are regularly <u>sampled</u> to check their quality. (___)
8. Many of the drinks industry's current problems <u>stem</u> from the bad weather in the peak sales season. (___)
9. External factors have a strong <u>influence</u> on sales in the drinks industry. (___)
10. The board took a calculated <u>risk</u> to appoint a man without management experience to such a senior post. (___)

3.3 Here is further practice on word classes, similar to the work you did in Ex 3.1. Use your dictionary to check the different word classes these words belong to.

Word	Word class
net	noun, verb, adjective
experience	
rates	
double	
essential	

Word	Word class
support	
ideal	
border	
prompt	
blame	

3.4   **Here is further practice on word classes, similar to the work you did in Ex 3.2. Which word class do the words in these sentences belong to?**

1. The Hilton's chief executive told bankers that the March 31st accounts would show <u>net</u> assets had risen to £635 million, compared with £385 million previously. (<u>adj</u>)

2. In the past five years, the company has <u>experienced</u> a sharp upturn in sales. (___)

3. The group <u>rates</u> very highly in all surveys of luxury hotels worldwide. (___)

4. The number of business clients has nearly <u>doubled</u> over the past five years. (___)

5. Easy access to the airport is regarded as <u>essential</u> by most business clients. (___)

6. We <u>support</u> the idea of building hotels in downtown business centres. (___)

7. The hotel is situated in an <u>ideal</u> location, which is convenient both for the airport and the nearby business centre. (___)

8. Furthermore, it is only a few miles from the <u>border</u>, making it a suitable venue for clients intending to travel by car to other countries in the region. (___)

9. Staff will always deal <u>promptly</u> with any complaints. (___)

10. The fall in business last year was <u>blamed</u> on the strike by air traffic controllers. (___)

Task 4	Review

4.1   **Complete these exercises about word class.**

1. Which word classes do these words belong to?

   a.   advanced, elementary, entire, normal, academic   _____

   b.   develop, prevent, avoid, provide, spend   _____

   c.   size, performance, explanation, security, existence   _____

   d.   frequently, particularly, basically, highly   _____

2. Which two word classes can these words belong to?

   a.   influence   ___ and ___

   b.   match   ___ and ___

   c.   joint   ___ and ___

   d.   lack   ___ and ___

4.2 **Complete the gaps to write a summary of what you have learnt.**

Knowledge of word class helps understanding of how to use _____ effectively. The best way to understand what word class a word _____ to is to read it in the context of a _____ or a paragraph. It is helpful to know that some words can belong to two or _____ word classes. For example, *prompt* can be a noun, a _____ or an adjective, and *spare* can be a _____, a verb or an adjective.

4.3 **Look again at the tasks in this unit and write down any new words or phrases you have learnt.**

Make sure you record which word class or word classes the words belong to. You may find it useful to record sentences in which the words occur.

Make your own notes here.

experience (noun and verb) – e.g., The company

experienced a downturn in sales.

_____

_____

_____

_____

_____

_____

_____

_____

_____

_____

For web resources relevant to this book, see:
www.englishforacademicstudy.com

These weblinks will give you access to tips on how to identify features of word class, an online article that outlines the different functions of a good **monolingual dictionary**, and reviews of several learner's dictionaries.

3 Word families and word parts

In this unit you will:

- build your vocabulary by learning different members of word families
- look at common **prefixes** and **suffixes** which are used to form different words, e.g., *~al* as a suffix to form adjectives like *parental*, *economical*, or *~ion* as a suffix to form nouns like *restriction*
- look at some common word parts which will help you identify the meanings of unknown words, e.g., *~port~* as in *export*, *portable*, etc.

Introduction

Read these sentences and note the different forms of the word *reduce*.

Of all the ideas for improving education, few are as simple or attractive as <u>reducing</u> the number of pupils per teacher.

Class-size <u>reduction</u> has lately developed from a subject of primarily academic interest to a key political issue.

The most obvious drawback to class-size <u>reduction</u> is the huge cost.

The state of California, for example, has been spending more than $1.5 billion annually over the past seven years <u>to reduce</u> class size to 20 or fewer for children in the four- to seven-year-old bracket.

Study tip

Learning vocabulary linked to one topic helps memorization.

Source: Ehrenberg, R. G., Brewer, D. J., Gamoran, A., & Willms, J. D. (2001, November). Does class size matter? *Scientific American, 285*(5), 78–85.

As you can see, two different forms of the word *reduce* are used here: the noun *reduction* and the verb *to reduce*. These words are part of the same **word family**. In these sentences, the different members of the word family are used to connect ideas within the text and make it cohesive. Knowing the different members of word families will give you another way of connecting ideas in your own written texts.

Look at another example of how different members of the same word family can be used to link together ideas and information in a text.

In this text, different members of the word family *child* are used: *child*, *childhood* and *children*.

As we showed earlier, attitudes towards **children** were changing, in the upper levels of society at least, by the seventeenth century, but **childhood**, as people think of it today, did not become clearly established for most of the population until the nineteenth century. Two key changes during this century were the restriction of **child** labour by the Factory Acts and the development of compulsory education, which was gradually lengthened until the school-leaving age reached 16 in 1972. These changes created a space for **childhood** between infancy and adulthood and kept **children** in the parental home for a longer period.

Source: Fulcher, J., & Scott, J. (1999). Sociology. Oxford: Oxford University Press.

Look at some of the other words from this text and their family members.

Word in text	Other family members
changes (noun)	change (verb)
restriction (noun)	restrict (verb), restrictive (adj)
lengthen (verb)	long (adj), length (noun)
development (noun)	developmental (adj), developmentally (adverb), develop (verb)
parental (adj)	parent (noun)

Notice that some of the family members look very different from each other, for example, *long* and *lengthen*. In other word families, the form of the words is the same but the word class is different, for example, *change* is both a noun and a verb.

Task 1   Words that do not change form

1.1   **Look at the verbs below and tick (✓) the ones which have the same form as the noun. If the noun has a different form, write it in the table.**

Verb	Noun: same form or different?		Verb	Noun: same form or different?
change	✓		respond	
restrict	*restriction*		influence	
employ			suggest	
cause			aim	
offer			argue	
depend			risk	
claim			waste	
decrease				

Task 2   Understanding word families through suffixes

In Unit 2 you looked at word classes. It is sometimes possible to recognize what class a word belongs to by looking at its ending, e.g., ~ion, ~ate, ~al, ~our, ~ive, ~ize, ~ly, ~ence, ~ity, ~ness.

Examples:

- *restrict**ion**, develop**ment*** = nouns
- *developmental, parental* = adjectives
- *developmental**ly*** = adverb

Note: Some suffixes provide meaning in addition to indicating word class. *Painful* and *painless* are both adjectives of the noun *pain*, but have different meanings.

2.1 **Put the words in the box into the table below according to their word class.**

~~activate~~   ~~appropriate~~   behaviour   calculate   development   difference
economical   equality   formation   gradually   realize   social

Nouns	Verbs	Adjectives	Adverbs
	activate	appropriate	

2.2 **Which word classes do the suffixes in the box suggest? Refer to Ex 2.1 and the Introduction to this unit and complete the table with suffixes which suggest word classes.**

~al   ~ate   ~ence   ~~~ion~~   ~ize   ~ity   ~ly   ~~~ment~~

Nouns	Verbs	Adjectives	Adverbs
~ion ~ment			

Note: Suffixes *can* indicate that words belong to a particular word class, but they are *not* a guarantee of this. One word that illustrates this is *appropriate* in Ex 2.1. Although it is most commonly used as an adjective, meaning 'suitable for a particular thing or cause', *appropriate* can also be used as a verb, as in 'to take possession of'. Other examples are the words *ritual* and *potential*. They both end in *~al*, but they are both used as nouns and adjectives.

Task 3	Understanding meaning through prefixes

In addition to suffixes at the end of words, which can indicate word class, we make use of prefixes at the beginning of words. These prefixes do not tell us about the class of words, but they can help us understand the meaning of words.

Example: *prerequisite, preconceive, prefix*

All the words above have the same prefix, *pre~*, which means 'before'.

We can remove a prefix from a word and it still remains a word. For example, the prefix *ir~* can be removed from these words: *irrelevant* (relevant), *irrational* (rational).

3.1 **Use your dictionary to complete the table with words beginning with the prefixes given.**

Prefixes	Example words
mono~	monotone, monorail
bi~	bipolar, biannual
re~	
inter~	
anti~	
geo~	
post~	
micro~	
semi~	
sub~	
thermo~	

3.2 **Look at the meanings of the words in Ex 3.1. Then match the meanings below to the prefixes from the table above.**

1. again, back   *re~*

2. after, later

3. exactly half, not complete

4. connected with heat

5. extremely small

6. between

7. under, a less important person or thing

8. connected with (the) Earth

9. against, opposed to

10. two, twice

11. one, singular

Task 4   Negative prefixes

Many words can be given a negative meaning by adding a prefix, for example, *convenient – inconvenient; agree – disagree.*

4.1   Check these words in your dictionary and see which of the following negative prefixes are used with them: *dis~, in~, un~, ir~, ab~, il~, im~.*

1. certainty   *uncertainty* _____
2. satisfactory _____
3. efficient   _____
4. likely   _____
5. appearance   _____
6. principled   _____
7. normal   _____
8. relevant   _____
9. legal   _____
10. moral   _____
11. published   _____

Note: In some cases, the prefixes *dis~, in~, un~, ir~, ab~, il~, im~* might create an opposite rather than a negative meaning. There are also some words beginning with these prefixes that do not have a negative *or* opposite meaning. For example: an *inbound* flight; to *implant* an artificial heart.

The prefix *in~* is not normally used with words beginning with *b, l, m, p* or *r.*

Task 5   Family members that look different from each other

When using a dictionary, you need to know how to locate the different words in a word family. The word under which a set of related words is located is called the **headword**. For example, when you look up *variation*, in some dictionaries you may find the word set: *varies, varying* and *varied.*

However, you won't find all family members in the same place in your dictionary. For example, you would have to look on a completely different page to find the following family members of *vary*: *variable, variation* and *variant.* If you want to find these family members, you would have to look at the stem of the word *var~.*

You can use this technique for many words, but sometimes words in the same word family can look very different from each other, e.g., *long (adj), length (n).* In these cases, you need to learn the related words and their spelling.

Note: A headword in a dictionary may have more than one definition, but only one entry. These words are **polysemes**, i.e., the definitions are related rather than completely different.

5.1 Match words from the left column with family members from the right column.

1. long (___)   ☐   a. poverty (___)

2. need (___)   ☐   b. obedience (___)

3. obey (___)   ☐   c. lend (___)

4. poor (___)   ☐   d. necessary (___)

5. loan (___)   ☐   e. length (___)

6. space (___)   ☐   f. description (___)

7. describe (___)   ☐   g. spatial (___)

5.2 Now write the word class next to each word in Ex 5.1: *n, v, adj*.

Task 6 | Complete word families

6.1 Complete the word family table below with the words in the box. There may be some columns where there are two entries. You may know some other words to complete the light green cells.

competition	decide	permit	economy
complicated	absence	certainty	competitively
original	competitive	complication	originate
decisive	permissible	economically	decisively
economize	origin	certainly	

Nouns	Verbs	Adjectives	Adverbs
	compete		
decision			
permission, permit			
		economic, economical	
			originally
	complicate		
		absent	
		certain	

6.2   **Complete the following sentences using a member of the word family given in brackets.**

1. Economists often argue that _____competition_____ is good for the consumer. (compete)

2. It is an absolute _____ that the ruling party will win the forthcoming election. (certain)

3. In the manager's _____, the assistant manager is in charge of the company. (absent)

4. Most people believe that high fuel prices are _____ damaging. (economy)

5. Photocopies of this certificate are not sufficient. The _____ documents need to be brought in. (origin)

6. The _____ to make 20 per cent of the workforce redundant was not taken lightly. (decide)

7. Photocopies may not be made without the _____ of the author. (permit)

8. The construction of the new road has been delayed as a result of legal _____. (complicate)

Task 7	Cohesion: using nouns and verbs to connect ideas

7.1   **In the following pairs of sentences you will need two forms of the same word. Use different forms of the words in this box to complete the sentences below.**

different	explain	difficult	argue	~~believe~~	develop

1. Supporters of Darwin's theories ____believe____ that human life evolved gradually over millions of years. This ____belief____ is strongly opposed by creationists.

2. The secretary _____ the registration process in some detail. However, the _____ was rather complicated and several people failed to understand.

3. People react in _____ ways to dangerous situations. These _____ cannot simply be attributed to psychological factors.

4. There is a strong _____ that there is a link between violent computer games and violent behaviour. The manufacturers of such games _____ that their products do not influence people's behaviour, however.

5. Some elderly people find pre-packaged foods
    _____ to open. The main
    _____ is that some of the materials
    used in packaging are quite tough.

6. Many studies have recorded how young
    children's language skills _____. The
    _____ of second-language skills in
    children is also of great interest to researchers.

Task 8	Word parts

In earlier tasks in this unit, we have seen that suffixes can give us information about *word classes* and that prefixes can give us some information about the *meaning* of words.

We can also find some **non-detachable word parts** which occur in a number of different words and which have related meanings. For example, the word part (or **root**) *phon(e)*, which means 'sound', is found in a number of different words whose meaning is connected to sound.

Examples: tele*phon*e, *phon*etics, micro*phon*e, etc.

Note: Non-detachable word parts cannot be separated from the word and still leave a complete word. For example, if you separate *mem~* from *memory*, what is left, *~ory*, is not a word. Contrast this with a prefix (see pages 24 and 25).

8.1 **Look at the groups of words below and <u>underline</u> any common word parts.**

1. <u>mem</u>ory, <u>mem</u>orial, re<u>mem</u>ber, com<u>mem</u>orate
2. centenary, percentage, century
3. transport, portable, import, export
4. biology, psychology, geology
5. television, telephone, telescope
6. visual, vision, visible
7. prospect, respect, perspective, spectator
8. photograph, telephoto, photosynthesis

> **Study tip**
>
> You will often find instances where word parts do not convey the meaning that they are usually connected to. For example, in *member*, *mem~* is not connected with 'keeping something in mind'.

8.2 **Use your dictionary to check the meaning of the words in Ex 8.1. Then match the word parts to their meanings.**

1. keep in mind   mem _____
2. light   _____
3. far away   _____
4. carry, move   _____

5. watch, look at _____
6. one hundred   _____
7. see   _____
8. study of   _____

Task 9   Review

Use this review section to develop your own learning strategies that you can use on a regular basis. The more you use them, the more automatic they will become.

9.1 **Look again at the tasks in this unit and write down any new words or phrases you have learnt.**

You may find it useful to write down phrases or sentences in which the words occur. You may also find it useful to write down the different members of the word family.

Example:

Word	Other members of word family
employ	employment, employer, employee, unemployed

Example sentences:

General Motors employs over 2,000 people.

Mexican law prohibits the employment of children under 14.

9.2 **Write a word family and example sentences for these words.**

1. compete _____

   _____

   _____

2. compare _____

   _____

   _____

3. direct _____

   _____

   _____

4. prepare _____

   _____

   _____

5. depend _____

   _____

   _____

9.3 **Add further word families and example sentences using words in this unit.**

_____

_____

_____

_____

_____

_____

_____

_____

_____

_____

_____

_____

_____

_____

_____

_____

_____

For web resources relevant to this book, see:
www.englishforacademicstudy.com

These weblinks will give you access to an online graphical dictionary, which uses coloured diagrams and mind maps to show how word families are linked together and a comprehensive series of lists clarifying the meanings of prefixes, suffixes and root forms, with example sentences and interesting exercises.

4 Collocations

In this unit you will:

- see how different classes of words combine in English
- learn some useful collocations

Introduction

Part of using a word properly is knowing what other words you can use it with. **Collocations** are the way that words combine in a language to produce natural-sounding speech and writing. For example, in English you say *tall person* but *high mountain*. It would not be normal to say *high person* or *tall mountain*.

Tall person is an example of an adjective + noun combination, but there are many other possible word combinations which we call collocations.

- *gain experience*   verb + noun
- *unemployment goes up*   noun + verb
- *interest rate*   noun + noun
- *rise sharply*   verb + adverb
- *choose between (two things)* verb + preposition
- *safe from (danger)*   adjective + preposition
- *in advance*   preposition + noun

Here are some examples in a text.

> Today most psychologists agree not only that both nature and nurture <u>play important roles</u> but that they interact continuously to <u>guide development</u>. For example, we shall see in Chapter 12 that the development of many <u>personality traits</u>, such as sociability and emotional stability, appear to be influenced about equally by heredity and environment; similarly, we shall see in Chapter 15 that <u>psychiatric illnesses</u> can have both genetic and environmental determinants.

Source: Atkinson, R. L., Atkinson, R. C., Smith, E. E., Bem, D. J., & Nolen-Hoeksema, S. (1999). *Hilgard's Introduction to Psychology*. California, CA: Wadsworth Pub Co.

In this text, you can see that the word *role* is used with the verb *play* and the adjective *important*. Knowing the words that collocate with *role* allows you to produce phrases like *play an important role*.

The other examples of collocations <u>highlighted</u> in the text above are:

- *guide development*   verb + noun
- *personality traits*   noun + noun
- *psychiatric illnesses*   adjective + noun

Note: For more on noun + noun combinations see Unit 5. Some noun + *and* + noun combinations have a fixed order. For example, you cannot write *nurture and nature*, or *figures and facts*; these should be written *nature and nurture* and *facts and figures*.

How do I learn collocations?

You already know many collocations without realizing it. For example, you will have learnt some of the following phrases in your earliest English lessons:

- *turn on the light*   verb + noun
- *have breakfast*   verb + noun
- *a beautiful day*   adjective + noun
- *ask a question*   verb + noun
- *Happy Birthday*   adjective + noun

In other words, you will learn many collocations without consciously studying them. However, you can *consciously* learn more collocations by looking carefully at texts or by using a dictionary.

Task 1	**Learning from texts**

1.1   **Read the text and answer the questions that follow.**

Note: The **stress** on the verb *pre<u>sent</u>* used in the text below falls on the second **syllable**, unlike the noun *<u>pre</u>sent*, where the stress is on the first syllable.

Because babies cannot explain what they are doing or tell us what they are thinking, developmental psychologists have had to design some very ingenious procedures to study the capacities of young infants. The basic method is to introduce some change in the baby's environment and observe his or her responses. For example, an investigator might present a tone or a flashing light and then see if there is a change in heart rate or if the baby turns its head or sucks more vigorously on a nipple. In some instances, the researcher will present two stimuli at the same time to determine if infants look longer at one than the other. If they do, it indicates that they can tell the stimuli apart and may indicate that they prefer one to the other.

Source: Atkinson, R. L., Atkinson, R. C., Smith, E. E., Bem, D. J., Nolen-Hoeksema, S. (1999). *Hilgard's Introduction to Psychology*. California, CA: Wadsworth Pub Co.

1. What verbs are used before the following nouns?

    a.   <u>*design*</u>   procedures   c.   _____ responses

    b.   _____ change   d.   _____ stimuli

2. What adjectives are used with these nouns?

    a.   _____ psychologists   c.   _____ infants

    b.   _____ procedures   d.   _____ method

Task 2	**Using a dictionary to learn collocations**

By studying the text in Ex 1.1, you can be fairly confident that the following phrases are good collocations.

- *design ingenious procedures*
- *observe someone's responses*
- *introduce a change*
- *young infants*

However, you may not know what other words you could use with the nouns above. For example, what other verbs could you use with *procedures*? One way of finding out is by using your monolingual dictionary. Some dictionaries give you specific information about collocations.

Word	Adjectives used with the word	Verbs used with the word
problem (noun)	fundamental, major, real, serious, etc.	face, solve, create, pose, etc.

With this information, you can be fairly confident that the following phrases would be correct.

- *pose a serious problem*
- *face a major problem*

In other cases, the information may not be given explicitly in your dictionary, but by looking at the example sentences in the dictionary you can identify collocations.

2.1 **Read sentences 1–9 and answer the questions below.**

1. Tom's family are putting *pressure* on him to accept the job offer.

2. There is great *pressure* on the UN to take action.

3. The government is coming under *pressure* to hold a public enquiry into the alleged corruption of some ministers.

4. I have no *doubts* at all about the new PA's ability to do the job.

5. Some people have expressed serious *doubts* over the government's economic policy.

6. There are still some *doubts* about the applicant's suitability for a senior position.

7. I am delighted to have the *opportunity* to present my ideas to such a distinguished audience.

8. There are now more *opportunities* for Eastern Europeans to find work in Western Europe.

9. I'd like to take this *opportunity* to thank you for your help in this matter.

Questions:

a. What verbs are used with the nouns *pressure*, *doubts* and *opportunities*?

_____

b. When *pressure*, *doubts* and *opportunities* are followed by a preposition and noun, what are the prepositions?

_____

c. When *pressure* and *opportunities* are followed by a verb phrase, what form does the verb take – 'to + infinitive' or 'verb + ~ing'?

_____

2.2 **You can use your answers to the different questions in Ex 2.1 to build phrases. Write out other phrases you can make by combining your answers.**

1. doubt

    have no doubts about
    _____

    _____

    _____

2. pressure

    put pressure on (someone to do something)
    _____

    _____

    _____

3. opportunity

    there is an opportunity for (someone to do something)
    _____

    _____

    _____

2.3 **Complete these sentences. All the words you need are in your answers to Ex 2.1.**

1. All the new supervisor needs is an opportunity _____*to*_____ show his ability.

2. Career opportunities _____ young people have improved in the last 20 years.

3. There _____ several opportunities for experienced programmers and software designers.

4. Sales managers always _____ pressure on their teams to achieve their targets.

5. The pressure _____ professionals in many walks of life is increasing day by day.

6. There _____ no doubt that sensible investment produces a good return.

7. I _____ doubts about the benefits of investing in gold in the present economic situation.

Task 3 Verb + noun combinations

3.1   **Use your dictionary to check which verbs are often used before these nouns.**

1. *make, have, cause* _____ trouble

2. _____ (a) business

3. _____ an effort

4. _____ an impact

5. _____ a connection

6. _____ an effect

7. _____ proof

8. _____ a gap

9. _____ standards

10. _____ concern

Task 4 Verb + noun + preposition combinations

4.1   **The verb + noun combinations from Ex 3.1 would also need a preposition if they were *followed by* a <u>noun phrase</u>. What prepositions would you need after the nouns in these sentences?**

1. The team are having a lot of trouble _____*with*_____ the new software.

2. There is a widening gap _____ rich and poor countries.

3. Tariffs on agricultural products have a major impact _____ farmers in the developing world.

> **Study tip**
>
> When you see a word you have been studying in an academic text or newspaper, think about the words it is used with. By taking an interest in words and how they are used, you will make rapid progress in vocabulary development.

4. There is a great deal of concern _____ the continuing drought in parts of Africa.

5. Another dry winter could have a serious effect _____ this year's harvest.

6. Some people fail to see a connection _____ subsidies to farmers in the West and poverty in the developing world.

7. Doing business directly _____ the people producing the goods is more cost-effective.

| Task 5 | **Adjective + noun combinations** |

5.1 **Look at these sentences and circle the adjectives that are used with the underlined nouns.**

1. The main <u>purpose</u> of the end of the month meeting is to set sales targets for the following month.

2. The sole <u>purpose</u> of the survey is to gather information to improve the quality of service provided.

3. Every single person on the project has been chosen for a particular <u>purpose</u>.

4. There is a growing <u>demand</u> for organic food.

5. In the past five years, there has been a huge <u>demand</u> for exotic fruit in the UK.

6. Recent <u>studies</u> show that the costs of importing food over long distances far outweigh the benefits.

7. Owing to the practical <u>nature</u> of the course, the number of participants will be limited to a maximum of 20.

8. It is human <u>nature</u> to want to be successful.

9. There is growing public <u>concern</u> about the high cost of public transport.

10. This issue will be discussed in greater <u>detail</u> in the next section.

5.2 **Use your dictionary to check which adjectives are often used before these nouns.**

1. *slight, dramatic, significant* _____ increase

2. _____ problem

3. _____ supply

4. _____ standards

Task 6   Adverb + verb, adverb + adjective combinations

6.1   **Underline the adverbs in these sentences and then answer the questions that follow.**

1. If natural resources were managed more effectively, the quality of human life could be improved.

2. Regular exercise can significantly reduce your risk of suffering a heart attack.

3. A balanced diet is especially important.

4. The maximum permitted daily dose is clearly stated on the label.

5. Some patients experience a recurrence of the symptoms as the effectiveness of the drug gradually decreases.

6. A knowledge of one or more foreign languages is particularly useful for market research positions.

7. It is becoming increasingly difficult to find people with adequate linguistic skills.

8. Online shopping is a relatively recent phenomenon.

9. The problem was probably caused by a computer virus.

10. Trojan viruses can spread rapidly and affect millions of computers in minutes.

11. The general manager strongly disagrees with the decision to replace all the hardware.

12. Using the new system is comparatively easy, and the basics can be learnt in just a few hours.

Questions:

a. Which adverbs are used with verbs and what verbs are they used with?

effectively – manage(d) effectively _____

_____   _____

_____   _____

b. Which adverbs are used with adjectives and which adjectives are they used with?

especially – especially important _____

_____   _____

_____   _____

Task 7   Review

7.1   **Complete these exercises using collocations from this unit.**

1. **Verb   +   Noun**

    _____   trouble

    _____   an effect

    _____   resources

    _____   a connection

2. **Verb   +   Noun   +   Preposition**

    have   trouble   _____

    have   an impact   _____

    do   business   _____

3. **Adjective   +   Noun**

    widening   _____

    sole   _____

    growing   _____

4. **Verb   +   Adverb**

    _____   significantly

    _____   rapidly

    _____   clearly

5. **Adverb   +   Adjective**

    _____   difficult

    _____   important

    _____   useful

7.2   **Look again at the tasks in this unit and write down any new words or phrases you have learnt.**

Make sure you record which word class or word classes the words belong to. You may find it useful to write down phrases or sentences in which the words occur.

Make your own notes here.

gap – e.g., There is a widening gap between the rich and the poor.

_____

_____

_____

_____

_____

_____

_____

_____

_____

_____

_____

_____

_____

_____

_____

For web resources relevant to this book, see:
www.englishforacademicstudy.com

These weblinks will give you access to a concordance, which lists every example of a word when it occurs in a large body of text – called a **corpus** – allowing you to see how the word is used in context; and a site that has a 'reverse dictionary' function (for when you know the definition but not the word).

5 Word grammar

In this unit you will:

- see how certain key words connect to each other
- see how these key words connect to the rest of the sentence

Introduction

When you study grammar, you learn about how different word classes behave in general. When you use individual words, however, you realize that not all words in the same word class behave in the same way. The way that words connect to each other and to the rest of the sentence varies from one word to another.

For example, there is one set of verbs that commonly occurs with *that* + **clause**, such as *think*, *say*, *know*, as in the sentence *Most people think that small classes help students learn more effectively.*

There is another set of verbs that commonly occurs with *to* + clause, such as *want*, *seem*, *like*, as in the sentence *Although the government wants to decrease class sizes, they are unable to find enough money to implement such policies.*

Task 1 Combining nouns

Academic texts are very rich in noun combinations, so it is important to understand the different ways that nouns combine.

1.1 Look at the following text and answer the questions.

> For many years after the discovery of America, the movement of free migrants from Europe was steady but quite small: transport costs were high, conditions harsh and the dangers of migration great. In 1650, a free migrant's passage to North America cost nearly half a year's wages for a farm labourer in southern England.

Source: On the move. (2001, May 10). *The Economist.* **Retrieved from http://www.economist.com**

1. What examples are there of two nouns (or noun phrases) connected by a preposition?

   Example: *the discovery of America*

   _____

   _____

2. What examples are there of two nouns connected using apostrophe (') + *s*?

   Example: *migrant's passage*

   _____

   Study tip

   Consult an advanced grammar book for comprehensive information about combining nouns.

3. What examples are there of noun + noun combinations without a preposition?

   Example: *transport costs*

   _____

Task 2 'Noun followed by noun' complement clauses

There are a number of nouns that are followed by *that* + clause. For example:

■ *It is my <u>belief (that)</u> the truth is generally preferable to lies.*
■ *Pasteur had a <u>theory that</u> many medical conditions were caused by viruses, bacteria and micro-organisms.*

Note: In the first example, *that* is optional and is therefore shown in brackets.

The function of the noun clause is to give meaning to the noun. As you can see in the two examples above, the clauses following the words *belief* and *theory* provide the content, or meaning. This is why they are called *noun **complement** clauses*.

2.1 **Read the following extract. Note that there can be other words between the noun and the noun complement clause.**

> ... the seventeenth-century British philosopher John Locke rejected the prevailing <u>notion</u> of his day <u>that babies were miniature adults ...</u>

Source: Atkinson, R. L., Atkinson, R. C., Smith, E. E., Bem, D. J., & Nolen-Hoeksema, S. (1999). *Hilgard's Introduction to Psychology*. California, CA: Wadsworth Pub Co.

2.2 **Use your dictionary to check the nouns in the table. Tick (✓) the nouns which can be followed by *that* + clause. Then choose two words and write example sentences.**

Word	*that* + clause
belief	✓
notion	
theory	
view	
idea	
fact	
suggestion	

_____

_____

_____

_____

3.1 **Look at the underlined nouns in the following sentences. Number each sentence 1–4, depending on whether the noun is followed by:**

1. a preposition (to connect the following nouns or **gerunds**)
2. *that* + clause
3. *to* + infinitive
4. *wh~* word + clause OR preposition + *wh~* word + clause

Write the number in the box provided.

a. ☐ 1   A new <u>system</u> for dealing with telephone enquiries has been put in place.

b. ☐   The prime minister rejected <u>claims</u> that he had acted without authority.

c. ☐   The <u>suggestion</u> that a new road should be built through the area did not go down well with environmental groups.

d. ☐   Over the past 35 years, <u>hundreds</u> of studies and <u>analyses</u> of existing data have focused on class size.

e. ☐   Many countries aspire to a more democratic <u>system</u> of government.

f. ☐   The <u>reason</u> why these laws are needed is to protect the public from violent individuals.

g. ☐   People give many different <u>reasons</u> for wanting to emigrate.

h. ☐   The increasing number of people living below the poverty line raises the whole <u>question</u> of the average wage and the standard of living in this country.

i. ☐   The purpose of the survey is to find more effective <u>ways</u> of evaluating job satisfaction.

j. ☐   Some companies set <u>limits</u> on the amount of money employees may claim for travel expenses.

k. ☐   There's no <u>limit</u> on the <u>amount</u> of money that can be exported from the country.

l. ☐   There is no <u>doubt</u> that penicillin is one of the most important discoveries in the <u>history</u> of medical research.

> **Study tip**
>
> A gerund operates in the same way as a noun, e.g., it can be the subject or the object of a sentence. It has the same form as the present participle, e.g., *smoking*.

3.2 **Look at the sentences you numbered *1* in Ex 3.1. Circle the preposition used to connect the underlined noun to the following noun or gerund.**

3.3   **Here is further practice in identifying noun patterns. Continue with the following sentences in the same way as in Ex 3.1.**

1. ☐ One <u>solution</u> to the spread of rabies is for animals to be vaccinated against the disease.

2. ☐ All <u>attempts</u> to control the spread of swine flu have failed.

3. ☐ Many people have a <u>suspicion</u> that the government is covering up the truth about the extent of the radiation leak.

4. ☐ There is a <u>risk</u> that the outbreak of E. coli may spread further and affect other parts of the country.

5. ☐ Regular exercise can help reduce the <u>risk</u> of heart disease.

6. ☐ Poor diet combined with lack of exercise is the <u>root</u> of many people's health problems.

7. ☐ You need formal <u>permission</u> to take copies of certain books out of the library.

8. ☐ The government has announced its <u>intention</u> to introduce a new peace plan in an attempt to end more than 20 years of conflict in the region.

9. ☐ The proposed peace plan includes a <u>mechanism</u> to share power between the two main parties.

10. ☐ The authorities have now examined the <u>extent</u> of the damage caused by the floods.

11. ☐ The <u>way</u> that some local people react to members of the traveller community varies greatly.

12. ☐ At the present time there seems to be no <u>way</u> to bring the two sides together.

3.4   **Look at the sentences you numbered *1* in Ex 3.3. Circle the preposition used to connect the underlined noun to the following noun or gerund.**

| Task 4 | Noun + noun combinations |

We have already seen three combinations of nouns without prepositions, in the Introduction and Task 1. Here are three more examples:

- *school subjects*
- *achievement levels*
- *classroom equipment*

Study tip

It is not possible to combine all nouns in this direct way, such as *school subjects* or *achievement levels*. However, noun + noun combinations are very common in academic texts.

4.1 **Use your dictionary to find more nouns that can be used in combination with the following nouns (either before or after).**

1. government   *figures, employees, spokesman, policy*

2. market   _____

3. computer   _____

4. problem   _____

5. company   _____

6. figure/figures   _____

7. rate   _____

Task 5   Adjectives and what follows them

As we saw in Unit 4, adjectives are used before nouns. However, they are also used in other positions and in other ways. Look at the way the adjective *important* is used in the following sentences.

- An <u>important</u> lesson can be learnt from this experience.
- Good health is more <u>important</u> than money.
- It is <u>important</u> to explain the risks of the operation to the patient.
- It is <u>important</u> that everyone understands the dangers of credit card debt.

In the first sentence, *important* is used before the noun. In the second sentence, it is used after the verb, but is talking about the noun *health*, the subject of the sentence. In the third and fourth sentences, *important* is used to comment on what comes after it, e.g., *explain the risks to the patient*. Another way of saying this would be: *Explaining risks to the patient is important*.

Notice that in the third sentence *important* is followed by *to* + infinitive, whereas in the fourth sentence it is followed by *that* + clause.

5.1 **Look at the underlined adjectives in the sentences below. Number each sentence 1–3, depending on whether the adjective is followed by:**

1. *that* + clause

2. *to* + infinitive

3. preposition + noun phrase

Write the number in the box provided.

a. ☐   Different vitamins are <u>necessary</u> for a healthy diet.

b. ☐   The new situation made it <u>necessary</u> to rethink the whole plan.

c. ☐ It's <u>difficult</u> to see how more money can be saved without cutting jobs.

d. ☐ It's rather <u>difficult</u> for me to understand the reasons behind John's behaviour.

e. ☐ The Internet makes it <u>possible</u> for many people to work from home.

f. ☐ It is <u>possible</u> that one day humans might live on other planets.

g. ☐ It has become <u>clear</u> that the situation is out of control.

h. ☐ It is <u>clear</u> to all of us that this matter deserves immediate attention.

i. ☐ The building of wind farms is <u>likely</u> to be unpopular with local residents.

j. ☐ It seems <u>likely</u> that supplies of natural gas will run out in the near future.

5.2 **Look at the sentences you numbered *3* in Ex 5.1 and identify the preposition used to connect the underlined adjective to the following noun phrase.**

5.3 **Look at the sentences in Ex 5.1 again. Check whether the underlined adjectives can be used immediately before nouns.**

5.4 **Use your dictionary to check these adjectives and answer the questions that follow.**

common	certain	customary
bound		useful

Study tip

Some monolingual dictionaries will give explicit information on how to use adjectives, e.g., with the adjective *familiar* you will probably find *familiar* (+ *to*). This means *familiar* can be followed by the preposition *to* and a noun or pronoun, e.g., *This place seems very familiar to me.* In other cases you can get information by looking closely at the example sentences.

1. Which of the adjectives can be used in this pattern?

   It is _____ for someone to do something.

2. Which of the adjectives can be used immediately before a noun?

   _____

3. Which of the adjectives can be used with *that* + clause?

   _____

4. Which of the adjectives can be immediately followed by *to* + infinitive?

   _____

Task 6 | Verbs and verb patterns

Verbs can also be followed by different patterns. Look at these two examples:

> In general, the ability to <u>distinguish</u> among smells has a clear adaptive value: it helps infants <u>avoid</u> noxious substances, thereby <u>increasing</u> their likelihood of survival.

> It is hard to <u>know</u> how much of the performance <u>stems</u> from other factors, such as a supportive home.

Source: Atkinson, R. L., Atkinson, R. C., Smith, E. E., Bem, D. J., & Nolen-Hoeksema, S. (1999). *Hilgard's Introduction to Psychology*. California, CA: Wadsworth Pub Co.

The underlined verbs in the texts above are followed by different patterns.

- *Avoid* and *increasing* are both followed by noun phrases – *noxious substances* and *their likelihood of survival*.
- *Stems* and *distinguish* are followed by prepositions + noun phrases – *from other factors* and *among smells*.
- *Know* is followed by a *wh~* word (*how much*) + clause – *how much of the performance stems from other factors*.

These are only some of the patterns that can be used with verbs. You will find other patterns as you study verbs in examples of text, or in a monolingual dictionary. For example, *know* can be followed by:

- a noun phrase
- a preposition + noun phrase
- a (*that*) + clause
- a *wh~* word + clause

> **Study tip**
>
> Individual verbs can be followed by different patterns. You have to learn which patterns can be used with each verb. You will find that by taking an interest in how language is used, you will start noticing these patterns.

For the verbs underlined in the extracts above, only the verb *know* can be followed by all of these patterns.

Task 7 | Transitive and intransitive verbs

Labelling verbs as transitive or intransitive is one of the most basic ways of categorizing verbs.
Transitive verbs can be used in the following two ways:

- With a direct object: *Many British children spend hours <u>watching</u> television.*
- In the **passive**: *Every week, rugby matches <u>are watched</u> by thousands of fans.*

Intransitive verbs <u>cannot</u> be used with a direct object and <u>cannot</u> be used in the passive.

- You can say: *It exists.*
- You cannot say: *It exists something.* OR *Something is existed.*

7.1 Look at the underlined verbs in the text and decide whether they are transitive or intransitive. Tick (✓) the correct column in the table.

> The surge of interest in smaller classes has <u>spurred</u> fresh analyses of the largest, most conclusive study to date, which <u>took place</u> in Tennessee in the late 1980s. At the same time, new data are <u>flowing</u> from various initiatives, <u>including</u> the California programme and a smaller one in Wisconsin. These results and analyses are finally <u>offering</u> some tentative responses to the questions that researchers must <u>answer</u> before legislators can <u>come up with</u> policies that make educational and economic sense: Do small classes in fact <u>improve</u> school achievement? If they do, at what age-level do they <u>accomplish</u> the greatest good? What kind of students <u>gain</u> the greatest benefit, and most importantly, how great is the benefit?

Source: Atkinson, R. L., Atkinson, R. C., Smith, E. E., Bem, D. J., & Nolen-Hoeksema, S. (1999). *Hilgard's Introduction to Psychology*. California, CA: Wadsworth Pub Co.

Verb	Transitive	Intransitive
1. spurred	✓	
2. took place		
3. are flowing		
4. including		
5. offering		
6. answer		
7. come up with		
8. improve		
9. accomplish		
10. gain		

You can use your dictionary to find out whether verbs are transitive or not. Different dictionaries use different symbols to indicate this. For example:

	Transitive	Intransitive
Oxford Advanced Learner's Dictionary	[VN], i.e., verb + noun	[V], i.e., verb
Longman Dictionary of Contemporary English	[T]	[I]
Macmillan English Dictionary for Advanced Learners	[T]	[I]

7.2 Look at the list of verbs below. Some are always transitive and some are always intransitive. Complete the table with these verbs. Then check your answers using your dictionary.

~~appear~~	belong	describe	~~include~~	interfere	lack
mention	~~present~~	remain	result	rise	suggest

Transitive	Intransitive
present include	appear

Note: Some intransitive verbs can become transitive if a preposition is added, for example, *result: A sudden change in temperature will inevitably result in rain.*

7.3 Check the verbs *belong* and *interfere* in your dictionary and complete these sentences with the correct prepositions.

1. The cars on display look as if they belong _____ a different era.

2. Anxiety can interfere _____ children's performance at school.

7.4 The following verbs are sometimes transitive and sometimes intransitive, depending on their meanings.

Read these sentences and decide if the underlined verbs are being used transitively (VT) or intransitively (VI).

1. The opposition is constantly questioning the prime minister's ability to <u>govern</u>.   *(VI)*

2. Bird flu quickly <u>spread</u> from animals to humans.   ____

3. Under the current economic conditions, the reform programme simply cannot <u>succeed</u>.   ____

4. People <u>tend</u> to save more money as they get older.   ____

5. A team of paramedics <u>tended</u> the most seriously injured.   ____

6. The jury <u>believed</u> the defendant's explanation.   ____

7. There are new laws which <u>govern</u> the import of animal products.   ____

8. Extra staff are being hired to <u>spread</u> the workload.   ____

Task 8   Verbs followed by *that* + clause

8.1   **Study the following example sentences.**

- *The IT team <u>argued</u> that they needed more money to complete the project.*
- *Both sides firmly <u>believe</u> that an agreement is now possible.*
- *Police now <u>know</u> that the crime was committed by someone known to the victim.*

Use your dictionary to check these verbs and tick (✓) which of them can be followed by *that* + clause.

Note: Good monolingual dictionaries normally give you the information explicitly, like this: <u>believe</u> [V (that)]: *People used to believe (that) the world was flat.*

Verb	*that* + clause
decrease	
behave	
state	
consider	
admit	
introduce	

8.2   **Read these sentences and underline any verb that is followed by *that* + clause.**

1. Smoking is widely believed to cause a range of medical problems.

2. Ten years ago it was finally agreed that tobacco advertising would be banned.

3. All the evidence suggests that the number of people smoking is falling steadily.

4. It is worth mentioning that teenagers in particular need to be warned about the dangers of smoking.

5. Some companies claim that their products can help people to stop smoking.

6. But some researchers have discovered that the chemicals in certain products actually increase nicotine dependence rather than reducing it.

7. In the US, smokers have come to accept that they can no longer smoke in any public place or workplace.

8. Some people have expressed concern about the widespread availability of cheap cigarettes from abroad.

9. The candidate admitted that she smoked even though the job description explicitly called for non-smokers.

10. Researchers claim to have discovered a harmless tobacco substitute.

| Task 9 | Verbs followed by *wh~* words |

By *wh~* words, we mean words that can be used to introduce direct questions, indirect questions or clauses after some verbs (but not all). The *wh~* words that can introduce clauses are:

- *who*
- *when*
- *whether*
- *where*
- *what*
- *why*
- *how* (even though it does not begin with *wh~*)

Not all verbs can be followed by these words and clauses, so it is important to learn which verbs can be used in this way.

Note: Sometimes it is also possible to use non-finite phrases after a *wh~* word, for example, *We learnt how to swim*. In order to use non-finite phrases instead of a clause, it is necessary that the subjects are the same in both, and the tense is the same in both. Compare the phrase above with *We are learning how the Second World War started*.

9.1 **Study the following examples of sentences followed by *wh~* word + clause or *wh~* word + infinitive.**

- There are websites specifically designed to help <u>businesses discover</u> what their competitors are doing.
- The police would normally ask the suspects to <u>explain what</u> they were doing at the time the crime was committed.
- Psychologists began to <u>ask whether</u> learning and experience play an important role in such differences.
- It is sometimes difficult to <u>decide whether</u> to invest money or save it.

9.2 **All the verbs in the table below can be followed by different *wh~* words + clause. Check the verbs in your dictionary and complete the table by writing in the appropriate *wh~* word followed by a phrase completion.**

Verb	*wh~* word	Phrase completion
doubt	whether	it is possible
consider		
determine		
explain		
decide		
describe		
realize		
discuss		

For the pattern used in Ex 9.1, the word order is not the same as it would be for questions introduced by *wh~* words. Compare the following:

Question:
What are our competitors doing?
wh~ word + auxiliary verb + subject + verb

Verb followed by *wh~* word:
(We need to) discover what our competitors are doing.
(complement +) verb + *wh~* word + subject + verb

9.3   **Rearrange these words to make sentences with verb + *wh~* words + clauses.**

1. will explain / The secretary / the forms / you have to / fill in / how

     The secretary will explain how you have to fill in the forms.

2. We / for next year / we want / to discuss / what kind of strategy / need

3. doubt / Many people / will live up to the promises / whether / made in the election campaign / the new government

4. are usually asked / for the position / The candidates / to describe / they would be suitable / why

5. The IT manager / should be updated / the system / whether / is considering / currently in place

6. People / have / what / with their own money / a right to decide / they should do

Task 10	Review

10.1   **Follow the instructions and write the words.**

1. Write three verbs that can be followed by *that*.

2. Write three verbs that can be followed by *wh~* words.

3. Write three nouns that can be followed by *that*.

_____   _____   _____

4. Write three adjectives that can be followed by *that*.

_____   _____   _____

5. Write three adjectives that can be followed by *to* + infinitive.

_____   _____   _____

10.2 **Look again at the tasks in this unit and write down any new words or phrases you have learnt. You may find it useful to write down phrases or sentences in which the words occur.**

Make your own notes here.

dissatisfaction – e.g., express dissatisfaction with _____

_____

_____

_____

_____

_____

_____

_____

_____

_____

_____

For web resources relevant to this book, see:
www.englishforacademicstudy.com

These weblinks will give you access to a comprehensive guide to verb patterns and a range of vocabulary quizzes.

Part 2: Academic Word List

In these units you will be studying the frequent word families which are listed in the Academic Word List Sublists 1–5 (see Appendix 1 for the full version of all the sublists).

You will look at the following aspects:

- Meanings of words
- Multi-meaning words
- Word classes
- Word families
- Collocations
- Word grammar

The first two tasks will establish the meaning of the words, before looking at them in more detail in a similar way to how you studied the General Service List words in Units 1–5 of the book.

Each unit ends with a word list containing words and phrases from the unit which occur frequently in academic English. These do not necessarily correspond with the Academic Word List in Appendix 1.

AWL – Sublist 1

In this unit you will:

- familiarize yourself with the word families in AWL Sublist 1
- practise understanding and using these words in context

Task 1 | Meanings of words

As you do the following exercises, pay special attention to the word class of each individual word.

1.1 **Study the underlined words in these sentences and think about their meaning.**

Education

1. The most obvious drawback to class-size reduction is the huge cost. It <u>requires</u> more teachers, more classrooms and more classroom equipment and resources.

2. Some studies have shown that the level of academic achievement amongst primary school children <u>varies</u> greatly depending on class size.

3. According to one source, the introduction of new secondary school examinations is <u>proceeding</u> smoothly.

4. Educationalists and school administrators are attempting to develop a common <u>approach</u> to controversial issues such as selection and streaming.

5. The growing popularity of Information Technology is <u>evident</u> in the numbers of students wanting to study it.

6. If a child is still doing well years later, it is hard to know how much of the performance stems from other <u>factors</u>, such as a supportive home.

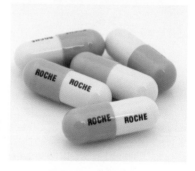

Health

7. There is no reason to <u>assume</u> that a drug that can treat this particular virus will ever be found.

8. Minor changes in the patient's condition can <u>occur</u> without any obvious external signs.

9. The number of drugs currently <u>available</u> to treat AIDS is strictly limited in certain parts of the world.

10. It is the medical researcher's job to <u>interpret</u> data gathered from thousands of hospital patients.

11. Most physicians believe we will <u>derive</u> great benefit from this new form of treatment.

12. He could see that the baby <u>responded</u> and was actively seeking his attention.

1.2 **Match the words in Ex 1.1 with the definitions on the right. The first one has been done for you.**

Word		Meaning
1. require	☐	**a.** to accept something as true, although you do not have proof
2. vary	☐	**b.** easily seen or understood
3. proceed	☐	**c.** to take actions or behaviours as having a particular meaning
4. approach	☐	**d.** able to be found, bought or obtained
5. evident	☐	**e.** to carry on doing something that has already started
6. factor	☐	**f.** a way of dealing with a situation or problem
7. assume	☐	**g.** to need something or someone
8. occur	☐	**h.** one of the things that causes a situation or influences the way it happens
9. available	☐	**i.** to obtain or come from another source
10. interpret	☐	**j.** to say or do something in reaction to something else
11. derive	☐	**k.** to change or be different in different circumstances
12. respond	☐	**l.** to happen

Study tip

The word *approach* is a polyseme, i.e., it has many related meanings.

The pronunciation of *proceeds* changes if you use the word as a verb or as a noun (pro<u>ceeds</u> = noun, pro<u>ceeds</u> = verb).

1.3 **Complete the pairs of sentences below with the words from Ex 1.2. In each pair you need the same word for both sentences. In the case of verbs, pay attention to the ending required, e.g., ~s, ~ed, ~ing. In the case of nouns, you have to decide whether the singular or plural form is appropriate.**

Health

1. Some of the most important vitamins required to stay healthy can be
    _____ from oily fish.
    The rapid spread of water-borne diseases in the town _____ from bacteria in the polluted rivers.

2. Kidney failure _____ in a very small minority of patients.
    Epidemics like bird 'flu _____ very rarely.

3. Some medical conditions are very serious and _____ urgent treatment.
    Any patient who _____ a special diet should inform the hospital authorities.

4. It soon became _____ from her appearance that Maria was seriously ill.

   It was _____ from the symptoms that she was suffering from an infection.

5. Medical experts believe that we need to _____ the problem of underage obesity in a completely different way.

   The _____ to preventative medicine vary greatly from country to country.

Business

6. Economists have _____ that the market will remain stable for the time being.

   We can _____, but not be certain, that more jobs will be created by the proposals.

7. Demand for particular products _____ with the seasons.

   Pay levels may _____ slightly, depending on relevant experience.

8. The board _____ the candidate's **reserved manner as rudeness.**

   The delegation will need someone to _____ **for them on their trip to Russia, as none of them speak a word of Russian.**

9. The recent increase in the number of redundancies is mainly due to social and economic _____.

   It is believed that tourism will be a key _____ in overcoming the current economic difficulties.

10. HRL is determined to _____ with its plans for expansion, despite the objections of local residents.

    We should define our terms before _____ any further.

Task 2	Multi-meaning words

2.1   **The underlined words in the sentences below have at least two meanings. Look at how they are used and choose the correct meaning.**

Engineering

Study tip

Multi-meaning words were introduced in Unit 1 and are called homonyms.

1. A prime example of globalization in engineering is in the Hyderabad <u>area</u> of India.
   - (a.) a particular part of a city, town, region or country
   - b.   the amount of space covered by the surface of a place or shape
   - c.   a particular subject or range of activities

2. The <u>issue</u> of whether or not engineers also need a degree in management is not yet resolved.
    a. to officially give people something to buy or use, e.g., a passport
    b. a subject or problem people discuss or argue about
    c. a magazine or newspaper that is published at a particular time

3. Governments need to <u>respond</u> to natural disasters with major infrastructure projects, such as road building.
    a. to react well to a particular kind of treatment
    b. to reply to something either verbally or in writing
    c. to say or do something in reaction to something else

4. It is important to consider safety <u>factors</u> because of the uncertainties in the design strength of structures.
    a. a particular level on a scale that measures how strong or large something is
    b. one of the things that causes a situation or influences the way it happens
    c. a number that can be divided evenly into another number

5. They are carrying out research to <u>establish</u> exactly why changes in the hydrological cycle are taking place.
    a. to start a new company or organization
    b. to secure a position by proving qualifications
    c. to find proof or facts that show that something is true

6. There is no one magic <u>formula</u> available for regeneration – each city requires its own development plan.
    a. the symbols, numbers or letters used to represent a rule in mathematics or science
    b. the step-by-step procedure used to solve a problem or achieve a result
    c. a list of the ingredients used to make things like medicines, drinks, etc.

Science

7. Natural resources such as sunlight, wind, rain and tides have become increasingly popular energy <u>sources</u> in the past 20 years.
    a. someone or something that provides you with something you need
    b. the cause of a problem
    c. a document or person that you get information from

8. A new science project initiated by a number of schools in the area has received full support from the local <u>authorities</u>.
    a. the power you have to make decisions or give other people instructions
    b. an official organization which has a specific area of responsibility for a region
    c. someone who is an expert in a particular subject

9. Generally speaking, materials expand when heated and <u>contract</u> with the cold.
    a. to become smaller
    b. to get an illness
    c. to formally agree to do something

10. Holding texts on computer enables a more scientific <u>approach</u> to the study of the language than has been possible up to now.
   a.   an offer or request to do something
   b.   getting closer to a point in time or space
   c.   a particular way of handling a situation or problem

11. One major problem is that scientific data can in most cases be <u>interpreted</u> in different ways.
   a.   to translate from one language into another
   b.   to explain the meaning of something
   c.   to take actions or behaviours as having a particular meaning

Task 3	Word classes

3.1   **Use a dictionary to check the following words. Then complete the tables with the word class they belong to, i.e., noun, verb, adjective or adverb. Some words belong in more than one class.**

Word	Word class
focus	*verb, noun*
benefit	
research	
policy	
individual	
function	

Word	Word class
assess	
specific	
finance	
consist (of/in)	
identify	

3.2   **Decide what word class would fill each gap in the following sentences. Write *v* (verb), *n* (noun) or *adj* (adjective) in the brackets after each gap.**

Education

1. The _____ (_n_) of recent research has been on class size.

2. Most found evidence that smaller classes _____ (___) students, particularly at the youngest level.

3. Every baby has his or her own _____ (___) personality.

4. Much educational _____ (___) is carried out using secondary or library data.

5. A new government might adopt a _____ (__) of reducing spending on higher education.

6. The technique is being tried in classrooms to _____ (__) what effects it may have.

7. In some _____ (__) age and subject categories, such as 17-year-olds and science, performance actually decreased slightly.

Business and Finance

8. Police are trying to _____ (__) the person responsible for removing over $2 million from personal bank accounts.

9. The banking and _____ (__) sector is growing at an astonishing rate.

10. The government used to have a policy which allowed banks to _____ (__) independently, free of external controls.

11. The alliance _____ (__) of a number of leading banks and financial institutions.

3.3 **Complete the sentences in Ex 3.2 with words from Ex 3.1. In the case of verbs, pay attention to the ending required, e.g., ~s, ~ed, ~ing. In the case of nouns, you may have to decide whether to use singular or plural forms.**

If you change your mind about any word classes while doing this exercise, think about what led you to the original conclusion.

Example: The __focus__ (_n_) of recent research has been on class size.

Task 4 — Word families

Look at these sentences and think about the relationship between the two underlined words.

A 'world car' may have the same 'platform', but is sold with different shapes, colours and accessories to meet local <u>requirements</u>.

Source: Understanding Global Issues. (1998). *The Global Village: Challenges for a Shrinking Planet* [Pamphlet]. Buckley, R.

Nevertheless, both regionalization and globalization <u>require</u> that more and more speakers and readers of local languages be multiliterate.

Source: On the move. (2001, May 10). *The Economist.* Retrieved from http://www.economist.com

The underlined words, *require* and *requirements*, are both members of the same word family. Other words in the two sentences also belong to word families.

Examples:

Word	Other members of the word family
different	difference (*n*), differ (*v*), differently (*adv*)
local	locality (*n*), localize (*v*), localization (*n*)

4.1 **Complete the table below with the words in the box. There may be some columns where there are two entries. You may know some other words to complete the light green cells.**

economy	economically	vary	analysis
definition	significantly	responsive	indicate
interpret	response	creation	creative
indication	environmentally	significant	variable

Nouns	Verbs	Adjectives	Adverbs
assessment	assess		
		economic economical	
variation			
	analyze		
significance			
		indicative	
	respond		
environment			
	create		
interpretation			
	define		

4.2 **Choose the correct form of the word in brackets to complete the sentences on page 61. In the case of verbs, pay attention to the ending required, e.g., ~ed, ~ing, ~s. In the case of nouns, you may have to decide whether the singular or plural form is appropriate.**

Health

1. The average daily food __requirement__ for an adult is between 2,000 and 3,000 calories. (require)

2. Life expectancy in some areas of Scotland is up to ten years lower than in other parts of the UK – a _____ finding from a policy point of view. (significant)

3. There continue to be regional and social class _____ in diet, and these can affect life expectancy significantly. (vary)

4. Statistics on obesity can be _____ in a number of different ways. (interpret)

5. A poor diet in infancy can _____ numerous problems in later life. (create)

6. It is difficult to provide an accurate _____ of a healthy diet, as this can vary from individual to individual. (define)

Environment

7. An _____ of data from Australia shows that the hole in the ozone layer over Antarctica is growing larger. (analyze)

8. The most recent _____ of the research suggests that human activities have had an influence on the global climate. (assess)

9. More recent studies _____ that ocean temperatures may rise by as much as 3°C over the next 50 years. (indicate)

10. Scientists have _____ by increasing the amount of research in this area. (respond)

11. The _____ effects of greenhouse gas emissions have been well-documented. (environment)

Prefixes

The following prefixes are used with a number of the words from the AWL Sublist 1.

Prefix	Meaning
re~	again, e.g., reheat = heat again
in~	not, the opposite of, e.g., *incomparable = not comparable*
un~	not, the opposite of, e.g., *unhappy = not happy*
mis~	bad or badly, e.g., *mistreat = treat badly*
over~	too much, additional, e.g., *overheat = heat too much*
under~	not a sufficient amount, e.g., *underfed = not fed enough*

4.3   **Which of the prefixes on page 61 can be used with the following words?**

1. variably   *invariably*

2. significant   _____

3. available   _____

4. create   _____

5. economical   _____

6. interpret   _____

7. responsive   _____

8. assess   _____

9. consistent   _____

10. estimate   _____

4.4   **Complete the following sentences using either:**
- the correct form of the word in brackets; or
- a prefix + the correct form of the word in brackets

In the case of verbs, pay attention to the ending required, e.g., ~ed, ~ing, ~s. In the case of nouns, you may have to decide whether the singular or plural form is appropriate.

Health

1. The government is concerned that health care is being managed in an
   _____ way and losing vast sums of money. (economical)

2. Some diseases mainly affect children but can also _____ in adults.
   (occur)

3. Because of the high prices, many cancer drugs are _____ in poor
   countries. (available)

4. Most doctors do not accept the government's interpretation because they say the
   results are _____ with the data produced. (consistent)

5. Compared with the problems people in the Third World have with diseases, our
   worries are _____. (significant)

Business and Finance

6. The business community recognizes that successful companies are those which are
   _____ to market changes. (responsive)

7. Financial reports can be _____ if people do not read them carefully. (interpret)

8. Numerous cases of online fraud have forced the major banks to _____ their security procedures. (assess)

9. The company _____ how much the project would cost and ended up spending £10,000 more than they had planned. (estimate)

Task 5   Collocations

Verbs and nouns

Look at these verb + noun combinations that appear in this unit.

Examples:
- *develop an approach*
- *derive benefit*

5.1   **Match the verbs on the left with the nouns on the right to make combinations from this unit.**

Verb		Noun
1. require	☐	a. effects
2. interpret	☐	b. research
3. meet	☐	c. the person
4. carry out	☐	d. requirements
5. adopt	☐	e. data
6. identify	☐	f. a special diet
7. assess	☐	g. a policy

5.2   **Choose the verb from the box that fits best with all the nouns in each group.**

adopt   ~~analyze~~   assess   create   define   establish   estimate   play

1. __analyze_____ data, results, problems, behaviour

2. _____ a role, a part

3. _____ a problem, a word, a term, a concept

4. _____ a plan, a strategy, a policy, an approach

5. _____ a company, the cause, the facts, a relationship

6. _____ cost, value, effects, the extent of something

7. _____ risk, performance, damage, effectiveness

8. _____ jobs, a system, a situation, wealth, products

5.3 Choose the noun from the box that fits best with all the verbs in each group.

an analysis	benefit	~~income~~	issues	methods	a theory

1. have, generate, supplement   _income_

2. discuss, address, raise   _____

3. use, develop, adopt   _____

4. support, test, develop   _____

5. do, carry out, give   _____

6. gain, bring, derive   _____

5.4 Look at the underlined words in the following sentences. Underline the verbs that combine with the underlined nouns to identify the different verb + noun and noun + verb combinations.

> **Study tip**
>
> You will learn a lot of collocations by paying attention to the way words are used together in texts.

Science

1. New <u>analysis</u> shows that the development of technology to remove carbon dioxide from the air would not be cost-effective in the foreseeable future.

2. The report provides a detailed <u>analysis</u> of the level of chemicals present in the water.

3. Scientists need to obtain more <u>data</u> before they can say for certain what the cause of the problem is.

4. All the <u>data</u> show that in the North Atlantic, hurricanes occur more frequently in the autumn.

5. The research involves collecting <u>data</u> from at least 20 random samples.

6. Some argue that there is little or no scientific <u>evidence</u> to support the evolution theory.

7. More <u>research</u> is needed into the long-term health risks of eating GM products.

Social Science

8. Recent <u>research</u> has shown that citizens are generally dissatisfied with the government's new approach to policing protests.

9. The prosecution failed to provide sufficient <u>evidence</u> to convict the accused.

10. After examining all the <u>evidence</u>, the judge agreed with the application.

11. If the government wants to crack down on crime, they need to adopt a much more radical <u>approach</u>.

12. There are several <u>benefits</u> you can claim if you are disabled and unable to work.

13. The introduction of the Jobcentre Plus scheme has brought many <u>benefits</u> to the unemployed.

14. Many studies of children's eating attitudes and behaviour have used the questionnaire <u>approach</u>.

Task 6	Word grammar

Discovering noun patterns

You studied the following patterns in Unit 5. Ex 6.1 will help you notice these patterns in the academic texts you read.

- noun + preposition, e.g., *function of*
- noun followed by *that*, e.g., *the theory that*
- noun + noun, e.g., *transport costs*

Note: For more information about noun patterns, see Unit 4.

6.1 **Look at the underlined nouns in the sentences on page 66 and answer the questions.**

1. Is a preposition used after the noun? If so, what preposition?

a. _____   b. _____   c. _____   d. _____   e. _____   f. _____

g. _____   h. _____   i. _____   j. _____   k. _____   l. _____

m. _____   n. _____   o. _____   p. _____   q. _____   r. _____

2. Which nouns are followed by *that* + clause?

_____

3. Which noun + noun combinations are used?

_____

Business and Finance

a.   The data supports the <u>theory</u> that higher oil prices lead to higher inflation.

b.   Chapter 5 discusses the <u>theory</u> of marketing costs.

c.   The <u>assumption</u> that money invested in the stock market will always make a rapid profit is a long way from the truth.

d.   Companies will need to make <u>assumptions</u> about the knowledge of their customers.

e.   There is clear <u>evidence</u> of a link between price reductions and increased sales.

f.   There is much supporting <u>evidence</u> for this belief.

g.   The study found no <u>evidence</u> that consumers are willing to pay a price premium for high-quality products in this area.

h.   The <u>function</u> of the sales manager is to maintain regular contact with all the company's main customers and to identify new customers.

i.   Both sides regard regular communication as fundamental to the <u>process</u> of maintaining a good business relationship.

> **Study tip**
>
> Noun + noun combinations are also called *compound nouns*.

Education

j.   The college is in the <u>process</u> of relocating closer to the town centre.

k.   Today's <u>approach</u> to teaching and learning is very different from 20 years ago.

l.   A systematic <u>approach</u> to grading students is beginning to take shape.

m.   Socioeconomic background is believed to be a significant <u>factor</u> in determining a child's academic success.

n.   The improved training scheme available in schools has been of great <u>benefit</u> to teachers.

o.   Students will be able to get maximum <u>benefit</u> from the extra-curricular activities.

p.   The <u>issue</u> of increased university fees has divided public opinion.

q.   The university has adopted a <u>policy</u> of requiring all students to have their own laptop.

r.   The government's new <u>policy</u> on education has generated a lot of criticism.

> **Noun + noun combinations**
>
> Here are some more examples of noun combinations from previous exercises in this unit.
>
> **Examples:**
> - *university fees*
> - *questionnaire approach*

6.2 Use the words in the box to make noun + noun combinations with the words in 1–4 below. You can place words from the box either before or after the words in 1–4.

analysis	collection	decision-making	decisions
findings	government	makers	production	team

1. policy   *government, makers, decisions*

2. research

3. data

4. process

6.3 Use your dictionary to find nouns that can be used in combination with the nouns in 1–5 (either before or after).

1. source   *energy, light, power*

2. labour

3. benefit

4. export

5. area

Transitive or intransitive verbs

In earlier exercises in this unit, we have seen examples of the following verbs which show that they can be used with noun phrases as objects: *analyze, define, establish, estimate, identify, assess*. All of these verbs are therefore transitive.

Examples:
- *Scientists are attempting to <u>assess</u> what side effects the drug may have.*
- *After years of research, scientists have <u>identified</u> the cause of the disease.*

6.4 The tables below show some other verbs from the AWL Sublist 1 that are always transitive, and others which are always intransitive. Complete the tables by putting the verbs from the box in the correct table.

~~assume~~	legislate	~~distribute~~	~~proceed~~	function	involve
issue	finance	occur	~~create~~	process

Transitive verbs	
assume	
create	
distribute	

Intransitive verbs	
proceed	

6.5 **Copy an example sentence from your dictionary for each of the transitive verbs from the completed table in Ex 6.4.**

distribute: Aid agencies are distributing food and blankets to the victims of the earthquake.

_____

_____

_____

_____

_____

6.6 **Copy an example sentence from your dictionary for each of the intransitive verbs from the completed table in Ex 6.4.**

proceed: Work is proceeding according to schedule.

_____

_____

Verbs that are both transitive and intransitive

The following verbs are sometimes transitive and sometimes intransitive: *approach, benefit, research, vary, respond, interpret, indicate.*

The meaning of a verb can change if it is used transitively or intransitively, e.g., *take off*: *He took off his coat* (transitive), *The plane took off* (intransitive).

6.7 **Look at the verbs as they are used in these sentences and decide if they are transitive (VT) or intransitive (VI).**

Language and Linguistics

1. The new government scheme will <u>benefit</u> language students from the EU. (*VT*)

2. Teachers must be ready to <u>respond</u> effectively to the needs of linguistically and culturally diverse children. (___)

3. The study <u>indicates</u> a strong connection between musical aptitude and linguistic ability. (___)

4. Sarah has been asked to <u>interpret</u> for the headteacher when the Russian visitors come to the school. (___)

5. Teaching methods may <u>vary</u> depending on the target audience. (___)

6. It is important for language colleges to <u>research</u> the market before setting up agencies overseas. (___)

7. As summer <u>approaches</u>, a large number of foreign students are expected to attend language courses in the UK. (___)

6.8 **Complete the sentences below with verbs from the box. Then decide whether the verb is transitive (VT) or intransitive (VI).**

estimate	include	to establish	define	is proceeding
involving	varies	require	indicates	has identified

Health

1. Health experts *estimate* that regular exercise can increase life expectancy by around five per cent. (*VT*)

2. Visitors to the country no longer _____ a vaccination certificate. (___)

3. Treatment _____ according to the seriousness of the condition. (___)

4. Research _____ that over 81 per cent of medical practitioners are dissatisfied with their salary. (___)

5. Doctors _____ a good patient as one who accepts their statements and their actions without question. (___)

6. The government _____ with its plan to move the hospital to another part of the city despite opposition from local residents. (___)

Business and Finance

7. The magazine _____ young women as a potential new market. (___)

8. The purpose of the questionnaire is _____ whether employees are satisfied with their current working conditions. (___)

9. Thorough marketing research will normally _____ the systematic identification, collection, analysis and distribution of information. (___)

10. Many companies are looking at improving their working practices by _____ all staff in the decision-making process. (___)

Task 7   Review

It is important you find time to review the exercises you have done in this unit and review what you have learnt.

7.1   **Look back through this unit and find:**

1. five noun + noun collocations

_____

_____

2. five nouns often followed by prepositions

_____

_____

3. five words that can be either nouns or verbs

_____

_____

7.2   **Look back over all the exercises you have done. Write down phrases that you think are useful and that you want to remember.**

Examples:

… the most obvious drawback …

… according to one source …

… there is no reason to assume …

… can be interpreted …

… research suggests that …

Make your own notes here.

_____

_____

_____

_____

_____

_____

_____

7.3 **Look at AWL Sublist 1 on pages 167–169. Check the words you don't know in your dictionary and make notes on the meaning and use of the words.**

Example:

Word (word class)	Meanings
constitutional (*adj*)	<ul><li>officially allowed or limited by the system of rules of a country or organization</li><li>connected with the constitution of a country or organization</li></ul>

Example phrases:

a constitutional right to privacy

a constitutional monarchy (i.e., a country ruled by a king or queen whose power is limited by a constitution)

a constitutional crisis

a constitutional reform / change / amendment

Other related words:

constitution (noun)

Make notes on other words here.

_____

_____

_____

_____

_____

_____

_____

_____

_____

_____

_____

_____

_____

_____

Vocabulary List

Business and Finance
bank account
business community
customer
exchange rate
fraud
globalization
inflation
localization
market change
marketing strategy
over-regulation
profit
risk
running costs
stock market
third quarter
uneconomical
value
wealth

Education
academic achievement
educationalist
higher education
school administrator
selection
streaming
study (*n*)

Environment
climate
emission
environmental issue
greenhouse gas
ozone layer

Health
AIDS
cancer
diet
disease

epidemic
infection
medical practitioner
medical researcher
physician
side effect
symptom
treatment
vaccination certificate
virus

Research
consumer
finding
questionnaire
random sample
statistics

Society
behaviour
class
constitutional monarchy
crime
infancy
life expectancy
regional
resident

Verbs
accept
address
adopt
affect
allow
carry out (research)
continue (to be)
deal (with)
depend (on)
gain
indicate
inform
invest

provide
raise
solve
stem (from)
suffer (from)
suggest
take shape
treat

Other
accurate
amendment
average
controversial
creative
crisis
decision-making
  process
detailed analysis
drawback
effect (*n*)
effective
external control
focus
freely available
fundamental
increase (*n*)
influence (*n*)
institution
leading
limited
minority
officially
opposition
organization
performance
point of view
popularity
practice (*n*)
project (*n*)
radical approach

rate
reduction
relationship
resources
right (*n*)
scientific evidence
statement
supporting
systematic
technique
well-documented

For web resources relevant to this book, see:
www.englishforacademicstudy.com

These weblinks will give you access to information and exercises related to the Academic Word List (AWL), and a series of interactive games and quizzes that enable you to test and expand your vocabulary for business and finance.

AWL – Sublist 2

In this unit you will:

- familiarize yourself with the word families in AWL Sublist 2
- practise understanding and using these words in context

| Task 1 | **Meanings of words** |

As you do these exercises, pay special attention to the word class of each individual word.

1.1 **Study the underlined words in the extracts below and think about their meaning.**

Health

1. People can be given special exercise routines that are <u>appropriate</u> for their needs.

2. It is wrong to <u>equate</u> weight loss solely with diet.

3. Physical exercise can <u>affect</u> one's health in a number of positive ways.

4. For a healthy diet, it is important to <u>restrict</u> the amount of fat consumed.

5. Swimming and weight training exercise quite <u>distinct</u> parts of the body.

Environment

6. Many companies are now hoping to exploit the <u>potential</u> of the Arctic region.

7. In contrast to weather, climate is generally influenced by slow changes in <u>features</u> like the ocean, the land, the orbit of the Earth around the Sun, and the energy output of the Sun.

8. There is a <u>complex</u> relationship between climate change and weather patterns.

9. The drought and <u>consequent</u> famine affected large parts of the country.

10. Global warming is not the result of one single <u>aspect</u> of human behaviour.

1.2 **Match the words from Ex 1.1 with the definitions on the right.**

Word

1. appropriate ☐
2. equate ☐
3. affect ☐
4. restrict ☐
5. distinct ☐
6. potential ☐
7. feature ☐
8. complex ☐
9. consequent ☐
10. aspect ☐

Meaning

a. made up of multiple parts and often complicated

b. happening as a result of something

c. to ensure something stays within a limit or limits

d. one of many parts of an idea or situation

e. a part of something that stands out as being important or interesting

f. to change or influence someone or something

g. the possibilities that something or someone has to offer

h. right for a specific use

i. obviously different or part of a contradictory type

j. to treat two things as equal or the same

> **Study tip**
>
> The difference between the use of *effect* (*n*, *v*) and *affect* (*v*) can cause problems for students. Check with a dictionary if you are unclear about the difference.

1.3 **Complete the pairs of sentences below with the words from Ex 1.2. In each pair, you need the same word for both sentences. In the case of verbs, pay attention to the ending required, e.g., ~s, ~ed, ~ing. In the case of nouns, you may have to decide whether the singular or plural form is appropriate.**

International Affairs

1. Emergency aid will be sent to the areas most _____ by the flooding.

   Extreme weather _____ many of the world's poorest regions.

2. The developmental needs of the new EU countries are quite _____ from those of the original member states.

   The European Union consists of 25 countries with _____ cultural, linguistic and economic roots.

3. Federalism and the Constitution are key _____ of American politics.

   One _____ of the American political system is the amount of autonomy each state has.

4. Few people understand the _____ issues of mass migration.

   The processes involved in eradicating poverty are very _____.

5. Developing countries need to maximize their _____ for economic growth.

    Fair-trade initiatives have the _____ to create many new jobs in developing countries.

Social Science

6. Some Western behaviour is not _____ in many other parts of the world.

    In some countries, people consider death to be the _____ punishment for possessing drugs.

7. The recent closure of several factories in Manchester and the _____ include the loss of jobs, which has had a severe effect on the whole area.

    Many people in the area are now unemployed, and as a _____, social problems are putting a strain on local resources.

8. In politics, some people seem to _____ openness with aggression.

    The Republican Party has always been _____ with right-wing policies.

9. Many countries have decided to _____ smoking in public places such as bars and restaurants.

    Smoking is _____ to designated areas.

10. This book deals with the social and religious _____ of Muslim societies.

    Religion is a major _____ of life in India.

Task 2	Multi-meaning words

2.1 **The underlined words in the sentences below have at least two meanings. Look at how they are used and choose the correct meaning.**

Social Science

1. An increased demand for <u>feature</u> writers has been prompted by the number of new magazines being published.
    a. a part of someone's face, such as their eyes, nose
    b. a part of something that stands out as being important or interesting
    c. an article given special prominence in a newspaper or a magazine

2. Manual workers are rarely given enough <u>credit</u> for all the hard work they do.
    a. an agreement with a company where a product is taken by a customer and paid for later
    b. appreciation or respect someone gets when they have done something well
    c. recognition a student gets from a college or university for completing a course

3. The <u>primary</u> objective of the new legislation is to raise standards of living.
    a. most important or fundamental
    b. the name given to the education of children between the ages of five and 11
    c. medically, the beginning of growth or development

4. Many teachers <u>maintain</u> that the latest changes in the curriculum will lead to a decline in educational standards.
   a. to allow something to continue as it had previously or at the same level
   b. to uphold a degree of action or motion
   c. to be certain that what you believe is correct

5. The police are <u>conducting</u> a thorough investigation into claims of racism.
   a. to carry out a specific project or task, particularly to find out information
   b. to transmit electricity or heat along or through something
   c. to take or show someone around somewhere

6. The government is trying to reintegrate mentally ill people into the <u>community</u>.
   a. society and the people in it
   b. an area and the people who live in it
   c. plants and animals that can be found together in a specific area

Economics

7. Developed countries <u>consume</u> huge quantities of raw materials.
   a. to make use of a quantity of something
   b. to eat or drink something
   c. to permanently use something up

8. This is made worse by the <u>range</u> of products demanded by the retail market.
   a. a set of items or people that are distinct but related
   b. the extent to which the quantity of something varies
   c. the group of products that an organization offers

9. There is an <u>element</u> of truth in the idea that creating wealth in society is good for the poor, but in reality they benefit very little.
   a. a substance consisting of only one type of atom
   b. one part of a complicated system
   c. an amount, usually small, of a quality or feeling

10. All <u>aspects</u> of the economy must be considered when reducing interest rates.
    a. many features of something
    b. the direction in which a window, room or front of a building faces
    c. how something or someone looks

Task 3	Word classes

3.1 **Use your dictionary to check these words. Then complete the tables with the word class they belong to, i.e., noun, verb, adjective or adverb. Some words belong in more than one class.**

Word	Word class
conclude	verb
acquire	
community	
relevant	
potential	

Word	Word class
resource	
transfer	
focus	
previous	
secure	

3.2   **Decide what word class would fill each gap in the following sentences. Write *v* (verb), *n* (noun) or *adj* (adjective) in the bracket after each gap.**

Environment

1. The article _____ (___) on recent research into the benefits of alternative medicine.

2. The study _____ (___) that sea temperatures are rising by 1°C every nine years.

3. Experts are attempting to identify _____ (___) risks to coastal areas from flooding caused by melting ice in polar regions.

4. Many of the world's mineral _____ (___) have already been exhausted.

5. The local _____ (___) plays an important role in the success of the new eco-friendly scheme.

Politics

6. The _____ (___) of power to a civilian government took longer than expected.

7. The government says that the arguments against hospital budget cuts are no longer _____ (___) in the current situation.

8. Many people feel less _____ (___) as a result of the sharp rise in crime.

9. The government is attempting to _____ (___) new powers to deal with violent crime.

10. The newly elected president reversed a lot of the policy decisions made by the _____ (___) president.

3.3   **Complete the sentences in Ex 3.2 with words from Ex 3.1. In the case of verbs, pay attention to the ending required, e.g., *~s*, *~ed*, *~ing*. In the case of nouns, you may have to decide whether the singular or plural form is appropriate.**

| Task 4 | Word families |

Look at these two sentences.

- *Some $15 billion was <u>invested</u> in the former Soviet bloc in Europe and Central Asia.*
- *Even North Korea, facing severe food shortages and economic decline, is keen to attract foreign <u>investment</u>.*

The underlined words are both members of the same word family. The word *invested* can also be used as an adjective, but in this word family there is no adverb.

4.1 **Complete the table with the words in the box. There may be some columns where there are two entries. You may know some other words to complete the light green cells.**

selective	complexity	normality	distinction
maintenance	computerize	strategic	regulation
participant	participation	resourceful	regional
perceive			

Nouns	Verbs	Adjectives	Adverbs
achievement	achieve		
		normal	
	participate		
	maintain		
perception			
	regulate		
strategy			
	select		
region			
resource			
		complex	
		distinct	
computer			

4.2 **Choose the correct form of the word in brackets to complete the following sentences. In the case of verbs, pay attention to the ending required, e.g., ~s, ~ed, ~ing. In the case of nouns, you may have to decide whether the singular or plural form is appropriate.**

Health

1. Contrary to popular _____, vigorous exercise is not necessarily good for your health. (perceive)

2. The _____ of medical practitioners in the decision-making process is absolutely essential. (participate)

3. The discovery of penicillin was one of the major medical _____ of the 20th century. (achieve)

4. A new _____ is needed to tackle the growing problem of AIDS in Africa. (strategy)

5. Some medical experts do not make any _____ between coeliac disease and wheat intolerance. (distinct)

Economics

6. Many believe that higher inflation is a direct _____ of the increase in the price of oil. (consequent)

7. The _____ of a stable and low rate of inflation is essential for economic development. (maintain)

8. The economy should be allowed to develop independently without the _____ of artificial government measures. (assist)

9. The government is often highly _____ in assigning funds to economically disadvantaged regions. (select)

10. Financial _____ in the public sector are very strict. (regulate)

Prefixes	
The following prefixes are used with a number of the words from AWL Sublist 2.	
Prefix	**Meaning**
re~	again
in~, un~, ab~, ir~	not, the opposite of
under~	not enough

4.3 **Which of the prefixes on page 79 can be used with the following words?**

1. secure _____

2. relevant _____

3. regulated _____

4. appropriate _____

5. construct _____

6. affected _____

7. normal _____

8. invest _____

9. obtainable _____

10. restricted _____

11. conclusive _____

4.4 **Complete the following sentences using either:**
- the correct form of the word in brackets; or
- a prefix + the correct form of the word in brackets

Health

1. An incorrect diagnosis of the patient's illness resulted in him receiving completely _____ treatment. (appropriate)

2. _____ information can often delay an accurate diagnosis of a patient's condition. (relevant)

3. Many hospitals are now allowing completely _____ access to people visiting patients. (restricted)

4. A body temperature of 40°C (104°F) indicates the presence of an _____ condition or symptom in the patient. (normal)

5. The patient received serious injuries in the accident but her vital organs were _____. (affected)

Business and Finance

6. The _____ of the buildings was funded by bank loans. (construction)

7. Make sure an investment broker is officially _____ and authorized before you hand over any of your money. (regulated)

8. Investment funds usually _____ their profits rather than pay them out to shareholders. (invest)

9. Zero inflation is an unrealistic and _____ goal for the economy at this stage. (obtainable)

10. The results of the investigation were _____, so the company's accounts will have to be examined again. (conclusive)

Task 5	Collocations

Verbs and nouns

Look at these verb + noun combinations that appear in this unit.

Examples:
- *(re)invest profits*
- *restrict access*

5.1 **Match the verbs on the left with the nouns on the right to make combinations from this unit.**

Verb		**Noun**
1. exploit	☐	a. investment
2. make	☐	b. an investigation
3. affect	☐	c. the potential of something
4. attract	☐	d. a distinction
5. conduct	☐	e. access
6. restrict	☐	f. one's health

5.2 **Choose the verb from the box that fits best with all the nouns in each group.**

~~achieve~~	affect	consume	design
evaluate	maintain	perceive	transfer

1. *achieve* _____   good results, objectives, high standards, success

2. _____   productivity, business, development, rates

3. _____   standards, quality, the status quo, interest

4. _____   needs, problems, threats, differences

5. _____   food, time, quantities, goods

6. _____   clothes, buildings, systems, courses

7. _____ money, funds, accounts, data

8. _____ effects, alternatives, effectiveness, evidence

5.3 **Choose one adjective from the box that fits best with all the nouns in each group.**

appropriate	~~complex~~	final	normal	positive	primary

1. _complex_ problem, relationship, structure

2. _____ objective, aim, function, purpose, concern, importance

3. _____ response, effect, influence, aspect, impact, experience

4. _____ decision, analysis, outcome, product, result, stage

5. _____ circumstances, practice, life, distribution, conditions

6. _____ action, time, response, manner, choice

5.4 **Look at the underlined words in the following sentences. Identify different combinations of verbs, nouns, adjectives and adverbs. Then answer the questions that follow.**

Information Technology

1. Technological advances are affecting every <u>aspect</u> of life.

2. Internet companies offer a vast <u>range</u> of products.

3. Software companies can provide a wide <u>range</u> of solutions.

4. The government has recently commissioned a <u>report</u> on cyberterrorism.

5. We can't upgrade the system until we have all the <u>relevant</u> information.

6. The use of the Internet to organize recent riots might have far-reaching <u>consequences</u> for some social networking sites.

Environment

7. The new research is particularly <u>relevant</u> to our environmental work.

8. Experts are trying to reduce the <u>impact</u> of the oil spill on marine life.

9. We need to focus on the environmental and ecological <u>aspects</u> of the problem.

10. Changes in energy policy will have a huge <u>impact</u> on the environment.

11. Volunteers were paid for their <u>participation</u> in the research.

12. The report makes a clear <u>distinction</u> between environmental concerns and environmental emergencies.

Politics

13. The government is looking at ways of increasing voter <u>participation</u> in elections.

14. The government's <u>regulation</u> of the Internet and media has increased considerably in the last few years.

15. The effectiveness of the proposals depends on how the authorities decide to enforce the <u>regulations</u>.

16. The government decided to lift <u>restrictions</u> on the export of foreign currency.

17. No currency or exchange <u>restrictions</u> are imposed on registered companies.

18. Politicians involved in the recent scandal have to face the <u>consequences</u> of their actions.

Questions:

a. What verbs are used with these nouns?

_____ impact

_____ regulations

_____ distinction

_____ restrictions

_____ consequences

_____ report

b. What nouns are used after these words?

aspect(s) of   _____

participation in   _____

relevant (to)   _____

regulation of   _____

range of   _____

c. What adjectives are used before these nouns?

_____ range

_____ impact

_____ aspect(s)

_____ consequences

d. What adverb is used before this word?

_____ relevant

Task 6	Word grammar

Discovering noun patterns

You studied the following patterns in Unit 5. Ex 6.1 will help you notice these patterns in the academic texts you read.

- noun + preposition, e.g., *distinction between*
- noun followed by *that*, e.g., *perception that*
- noun + noun, e.g., *population growth*

6.1 **Look at the underlined nouns in the sentences below and answer the following questions.**

1. Is a preposition used after the noun? If so, what preposition?

a. _____ b. _____ c. _____ d. _____ e. _____ f. _____

g. _____ h. _____ i. _____ j. _____ k. _____ l. _____

m. _____ n. _____

2. Which nouns are followed by *that* + clause? _____

Health

a. It is vital to understand the <u>distinction</u> between bacterial infections and viral infections.
b. We need to assess the potential <u>impact</u> of avian flu on the human population.
c. The <u>focus</u> of the conference shifted from population growth to the eradication of common diseases.
d. There is a widespread <u>perception</u> that antiviral drugs can be developed quickly.
e. The <u>relevance</u> of this concept to physicians is discussed in theoretical terms in this chapter.
f. The <u>restrictions</u> on importing drugs are designed to limit the potential <u>impact</u> of unlicensed drugs on the local market.

Sport

g. The test measures children's <u>achievements</u> in different sports.

h. The sporting <u>achievements</u> of the team captain have been recorded in a new book.

i. Active <u>participation</u> in sporting activities is a requirement for most young children.

j. The emphasis is on <u>participation</u> by teenagers and young adults in local projects.

k. The <u>emphasis</u> is on the success of the team rather than on the <u>achievement</u> of individual players.

Environment

l. The <u>acquisition</u> of the woodland is being investigated by the Forestry Commission.

m. If sea levels continue to rise, it will have very serious <u>consequences</u> for many cities in low-lying areas.

n. More extreme weather conditions are the unavoidable <u>consequences</u> of global warming.

Noun + noun combinations

Here are some more examples of noun + noun combinations from Ex 5.4.
- *voter participation* (sentence 13)
- *exchange restrictions* (sentence 17)

6.2 Use the words in the box to make noun + noun combinations with the words in 1–4 below. Words from the box might come before or after the words in 1–4.

consumption	computer	construction	restrictions

1. energy, food, fuel, alcohol _____

2. system, screen, software, programmer, industry _____

3. manager, industry, work, company _____

4. speed, trade, travel, import _____

6.3 Use your dictionary to find nouns that can be used in combination with the nouns in 1–4 (either before or after).

1. review _____

2. regulations _____

3. security _____

4. administrators _____

Note: For more information about noun patterns, see Unit 5.

Transitive or intransitive verbs

In earlier exercises in this unit, we have seen examples of the following verbs which show that they can be used with noun phrases as objects: *affect, achieve, acquire, conduct, construct, consume, invest, maintain, restrict.* All of these verbs are therefore transitive.

Example:

- *Environmental factors can <u>affect</u> human development before birth.*

6.4 The tables below show some other verbs from AWL Sublist 2 that are always transitive and others that are always intransitive. Complete the tables by putting the verbs from the box in the correct column.

credit	~~participate~~	feature	~~categorize~~	select
~~design~~	regulate	~~purchase~~	~~seek~~	finalize
survey	~~evaluate~~	regulate	~~equate~~	reside
	~~injure~~		perceive	

Transitive verbs			Intransitive verbs	
categorize			participate	
equate				
evaluate				
design				
injure				
purchase				
seek				

6.5 Copy an example sentence from your dictionary for each of the transitive verbs from the completed table in Ex 6.4.

Note: See Unit 5 for more on transitive and intransitive verbs.

<u>categorize</u>: *The population is <u>categorized</u> according to age, sex and social group.*

6.6   **Copy an example sentence from your dictionary for each of the intransitive verbs from the completed table in Ex 6.4.**

participate: Everyone in the class is expected _to participate_ actively in these discussions.

Verbs that are both transitive and intransitive
The following verbs are sometimes transitive and sometimes intransitive: _assist, conclude, focus, transfer, obtain, impact._

6.7 **Look at the verbs as they are used in these sentences and decide if they are transitive (VT) or intransitive (VI).**

Business

1. This leaflet will <u>assist</u> consumers in selecting the best insurance policy. (___)

2. The report <u>concludes</u> with references to the rise in inflation and the decline in business optimism. (___)

3. Ideas that work well in one business situation may not <u>transfer</u> well to another. (___)

4. The research project will <u>focus</u> on the impact of e-business on an organization. (___)

5. The purpose of the research is to identify problem areas and to <u>obtain</u> objective data for analysis. (___)

6. The new law will progressively <u>impact</u> on the way businesses operate. (___)

Task 7	Review

It is important you find time to review the exercises you have done in this unit and review what you have learnt.

7.1 **Look back through this unit and find:**

1. five adjective + noun collocations

_____

_____

_____

_____

_____

2. five noun + noun collocations

_____

_____

_____

_____

_____

3. five nouns often followed by prepositions

_____

_____

_____

_____

_____

4. five words that can be either nouns or verbs

_____

_____

_____

_____

_____

7.2 **Look back over all the exercises you have done and write down phrases that you think are useful and that you want to remember.**

Examples:

… it is wrong to equate …

… in contrast to …

… the primary objective of …

… conduct a thorough investigation into …

… may contain an element of truth …

… make a distinction between …

Make your own notes here.

_____

_____

_____

_____

_____

_____

_____

_____

_____

7.3 **Look at AWL Sublist 2 on pages 170–171. Check the words you don't know in your dictionary and make notes on the meaning and use of the words.**

Example notes:

Word (word class)	Meanings
item (*n*)	■ a single thing, especially one thing in a list, group or set of things ■ a single, usually short, piece of news in a newspaper or magazine, or on television

Example phrases:

an item of clothing / furniture / jewellery

an item on the agenda / list / menu

luxury items

a news item

Other related words:

itemize (transitive verb)

Make your own notes here.

Vocabulary List

Business and Finance
bank loan
business optimism
developed country
developing country
development (of)
disadvantaged
economic decline
economic growth
exchange restriction
fair-trade initiative
foreign investment
funds
insurance policy
investment broker
investment fund
productivity
raw materials
retail market
shareholder
zero inflation

Education
educational standards

Environment
Arctic region
climate change
coastal area
developmental needs
emergency aid
energy output
extreme weather
famine
flooding
Forestry Commission
global warming
low-lying area

marine life
mineral resources
oil spill
orbit
polar region
sea level
weather pattern

Health
avian flu
bacterial infection
body temperature
cloning
diagnosis
exercise routine
health and safety
healthy diet
mentally ill
penicillin
physical exercise
vigorous exercise
viral infection
vital organ
weight loss
weight training

Politics
civilian government
election
European Union (EU)
federalism
government measure
legislation
member state
newly elected
policy decision
Soviet bloc
voter participation

Research
objective data

Society
local resources
population growth
public place
punishment
religious
social group
social problem
suspect (n)
investigation
unemployed
violent crime

Verbs
assign
attempt
attract (investment)
exhaust
exploit (the potential of)
hand over
influence
make (a distinction)
maximize
possess
register
reintegrate
reverse
tackle

Other
according to
argument
artificial
authorized
belief
circumstances

contrary to (popular
　opinion)
designated area
distinction
element of truth (an ~)
essential
far-reaching
　consequences
feature writer
in contrast to
linguistic
presence
primary objective
progressively
relevant information
severe effect
standardized
strain
theoretical
unavoidable
　consequences
volunteer (n)
widespread perception

For web resources relevant to this book, see:
www.englishforacademicstudy.com

These weblinks will give you access to authentic news items, with transcripts of the broadcasts in order to focus on key vocabulary and the way it is used; and useful information on how to learn English vocabulary in an academic context.

AWL – Sublist 3

In this unit you will:

- familiarize yourself with the word families in AWL Sublist 3
- practise understanding and using these words in context

Task 1   Meanings of words

As you do these exercises, pay special attention to the word class of each individual word.

1.1   **Study the underlined words in the extracts below and think about their meaning.**

Manufacturing

1. The machine consists of more than two hundred different <u>components</u>.

2. It is fully guaranteed for a period of five years, <u>excluding</u> electrical parts.

3. Its <u>initial</u> performance should match the criteria set out in the technical specifications.

4. Any operator mishandling of the machine may <u>constrain</u> the right of the customer to claim replacement components.

5. The manufacturer retains the right to refuse <u>consent</u> for repair work if the terms of the contract have been broken.

Science

6. Darwin's observations led him to <u>deduce</u> that animals could adapt to their surroundings.

7. The <u>dominant</u> male baboon is the largest in the group.

8. In certain groups of apes and other primates, there is a <u>core</u> of animals which enjoy greater power than the other members of the group.

9. Ape society seems to consist of different <u>layers</u> of seniority.

10. At the moment, it's impossible to say for sure what the <u>outcome</u> of the research will be.

1.2   **Match the words from Ex 1.1 with the definitions on the right.**

Word		Meaning
1. component	☐	a. to produce an opinion as a result of information
2. excluding	☐	b. stronger or more obvious than other people or things which are similar
3. initial	☐	c. to allow something to happen
4. constrain	☐	d. happening when something first starts

Word		Meaning
5. consent	☐	e. the strongest members of a group
6. deduce	☐	f. one of the many parts that make up a machine or system
7. dominant	☐	g. the results or consequences of something
8. core	☐	h. to prevent or limit something
9. layer	☐	i. not including
10. outcome	☐	j. one of several levels within an organization

1.3   **Complete the pairs of sentences below with the words from Ex 1.2. In each pair, you need the same word for both sentences. In the case of verbs, pay attention to the ending required, e.g., ~s, ~ed, ~ing. In the case of nouns, you may have to decide whether the singular or plural form is appropriate.**

Engineering

1. The truck frame is the principal _____ of a forklift truck.
    The factory makes car engine _____.

2. Carter Construction _____ the construction industry in the past.
    Ten years ago, the company enjoyed a _____ share of the market.

3. The _____ stage of the project is to build the transport infrastructure.
    _____ safety checks will be carried out before the main phase of the construction project begins.

4. Planning regulations _____ building development in the past.
    The hospital does not want financial problems to _____ the building of new medical facilities.

5. _____ the cost of hiring local machine operators, the construction project cost over $1.5 million.
    The contract drawn up for the road improvement project _____ insurance.

Environment

6. Carbon dating procedures enable scientists to _____ the probable age of ancient remains.

   Scientists have _____ from observing shellfish fossils that the area had once been covered in water.

7. A large hole in the ozone _____ has appeared over Antarctica.

   The Welsh coastline is made up of several different _____ of rock.

8. Geophysicists study the Earth's _____ as well as the movement of tectonic plates.

   Scientists can measure how much carbon dioxide was present in the atmosphere thousands of years ago by studying the _____ at the centre of ice in the Arctic Circle.

9. Environmental campaigners hoped for a positive _____ to the UN's climate change summit.

   The government's new Energy Bill has had several _____.

10. The water company will need written _____ from the Environment Agency before they dig up pipes near the river.

    The Environment Agency had not _____ to flood defences being built next to the river, so these had to be demolished.

Task 2	Multi-meaning words

2.1 **The underlined words in the sentences below have at least two meanings. Look at how they are used and choose the correct meaning.**

1. The temperature at the Earth's <u>core</u> is believed to be between 3,000 and 5,000°C.
   a. the hard central part of a fruit such as an apple that contains the seeds
   b. the strongest, most supportive members of a group
   c. the middle of a planet

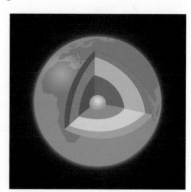

2. A number of different human activities have <u>contributed</u> to climate change.
   a. to add your money, goods, ideas or time and effort to something
   b. to be one of the reasons that something happens
   c. to have written for a newspaper or magazine

Science

3. The studies clearly <u>demonstrate</u> the link between fossil fuels and climate change.
   a. to show something is true
   b. to show another person how to do something by doing it yourself
   c. to protest against or support something with other people in a public place

4. The earthquake <u>registered</u> 6.9 on the Richter scale.
   a. to enter someone's name on an official list
   b. to give your opinion about something officially so that everyone knows your feelings
   c. to show as a measurement on a piece of equipment

Economics

5. Although prices of most basic commodities have risen in the past year, some have remained <u>constant</u>.
   a. of a regular nature over a period of time
   b. remaining at the same level or amount
   c. loyal to a person or friend

6. The red sector in the pie chart <u>corresponds</u> to monthly expenditure on food.
   a. to be like something else or very similar to it
   b. to exchange letters with someone regularly
   c. to relate or link to something

7. People have perfectly <u>valid</u> reasons for being concerned about the long-term effects of the recession.
   a. a ticket or document which is officially acceptable
   b. a reasonable argument that most people would accept
   c. a user name or password that will be accepted by a computer system

8. The data <u>implies</u> that inflation rates might fall next year.
   a. to suggest that something is likely to exist or to be true
   b. to suggest that you think something without expressing it directly

9. The graph clearly <u>illustrates</u> the inflation trend over the past two years.
   a. to explain something by referring to something visual, such as a picture, diagram or graph
   b. to be an example which shows that something is correct or factual
   c. to create artwork for a book, magazine article, etc.

Social Science

10. There has been an enormous <u>shift</u> in attitudes towards smoking during the past 20 years.
    a. a change in something
    b. a period of work time in a factory
    c. a key on a computer keyboard

11. Employees in this country pay up to 40 per cent of their income in tax and other <u>deductions</u>.
    a. using evidence or information in order to understand something
    b. the amount that is subtracted from a total, or the process of subtraction

12. Many people feel that the government's benefit cuts cannot be <u>justified</u>.
 a. to show there is a good explanation for something that other people may think is unreasonable
 b. to give an acceptable reason for something
 c. to make the left or right edges of a piece of writing straight on a page

13. A <u>fund</u> has been set up to help finance small start-up companies.
 a. a supply of money that people collect and keep for a specific reason
 b. a large amount of something which is usually useful

14. Human rights activists believe the government should <u>compensate</u> victims of abuse by police and armed forces personnel.
 a. to balance the effect of something negative
 b. to pay someone money for an injury or loss

Task 3   Word classes

3.1   **Use your dictionary to check these words. Then complete the tables with the word class they belong to, i.e., noun, verb, adjective or adverb. Some words belong to more than one class.**

Word	Word class	Word	Word class
shift	*noun, verb*	consent	
link		minority	
proportion		register	
sequence		specify	
volume		comment	
alternative		emphasize	

3.2   **Decide what word class would fill each gap in the following sentences. Write *v* (verb), *n* (noun) or *adj* (adjective) in the brackets after each gap.**

Science

1. The 18th-century chemist Jacques Charles studied the relationship between the _____ (___) of gas and temperature.

2. Virtually all children go through the same _____ (___) of motor behaviours in the same order.

3. Scientists have _____ (___) environmental factors with the development of unborn babies.

4. The theory of evolution _____ (___) the biological basis of human development.

5. A high _____ (___) of babies born to mothers who were smokers have a less than average body weight at birth.

6. The book details _____ (___) ways to bring up young children.

Health

7. Patients have the right to refuse _____ (___) for a particular treatment at any time.

8. Journalists often ask doctors about the health of famous patients, but they usually refuse to _____ (___).

9. Manufacturers of pharmaceuticals have to _____ (___) clearly which side effects patients might experience.

10. Employees from ethnic _____ (___) account for up to 40 per cent of the total number of health workers in certain areas of the country.

11. All patients must be _____ (___) on arrival at the hospital.

12. Once again, scientists are _____ (___) their focus back towards a virus as the most likely cause of the problem.

3.3 **Now complete the sentences in Ex 3.2 with words from Ex 3.1. In the case of verbs, pay attention to the ending required, e.g., ~s, ~ed, ~ing. In the case of nouns, you may have to decide whether the singular or plural form is appropriate.**

| Task 4 | Word families |

Look at these two sentences.

> Many governments began trying to control <u>immigration</u>.

> The numbers of legal and illegal <u>immigrants</u> grew nonetheless, as economics had its way.

Source: On the move. (2001, May 10). *The Economist*. Retrieved from http://www.economist.com

The underlined words are both members of the same word family, and the writer uses them to make the writing more cohesive.

Complete the table with these words. There may be some columns where there are two entries. You may be able to complete the light green cells with some other words you know.

exclusively   alternatively   compensation   constantly

constraint   proportional   contribution   validity

correspondingly   sufficiently   deduction   reliable

illustrate   reliability   initially   reliance

locate   specific   justification   emphasize   implication

Nouns	Verbs	Adjectives	Adverbs
reaction	react		
validation			
	specify		
	rely		
illustration			
location			
	justify		
	imply		
		initial	
	correspond		
		alternative	
	compensate		
	contribute		
		constant	
	constrain		
	deduce		

Nouns	Verbs	Adjectives	Adverbs
		exclusive	
proportion			
		sufficient	
emphasis			

4.2 **Choose the correct form of the word in brackets to complete the following sentences. In the case of verbs, pay attention to the ending required, e.g., ~s, ~ed, ~ing. In the case of nouns, you may have to decide whether the singular or plural form is more appropriate.**

Business and Finance

1. The government will pay full _____ to businesses affected by the new regulation. (compensate)

2. Microsoft has decided to place greater _____ on developing new products. (emphasize)

3. _____, we had planned to focus solely on the domestic market. (initial)

4. However, the unfavourable _____ of many overseas customers to our latest range forced us to change our strategy. (react)

5. Focusing on research and development will have _____ for short-term profitability. (imply)

Language and Linguistics

6. Diagnostic tests are usually run by teachers to identify _____ language points that need to be reviewed. (specify)

7. It usually requires many years to learn a language _____ well in order to be able to speak fluently. (sufficient)

8. In order to remember new vocabulary, learners need to _____ review the words they have learnt in class. (constant)

9. You can learn a language by attending a course, or _____ by living in the country where the language is spoken. (alternative)

10. The learners' _____ in lessons are key to their success. (contribute)

Prefixes	
The following prefixes are used with a number of the words from AWL Sublist 3.	
Prefix	**Meaning**
re~	again
in~, un~, dis~, de~	not, the opposite of

4.3 **Which of the above prefixes can be used with the following words?**

1. validate   _____

2. sufficient   _____

3. specified   _____

4. reliable   _____

5. proportionate   _____

6. locate   _____

7. justified   _____

8. conventional   _____

4.4 **Complete the following sentences using either:**
- the correct form of the word in brackets; or
- a prefix + the correct form of the word in brackets

In the case of verbs, pay attention to the ending required, e.g., *~ed, ~ing, ~s.*

Research

1. Statistics can sometimes be _____ and lead to overgeneralized conclusions. (reliable)

2. The conclusions of the report are _____ by the low number of people in the survey. (validate)

3. If the amount of data available is _____, the study cannot be conducted properly. (sufficient)

4. The high level of crime in the city has forced the company to _____ to a rural area. (locate)

5. The study reveals that 80 per cent of complaints were _____ and a waste of police time. (justify)

Task 5	Collocations

Verbs and nouns

Look at these verb + noun combinations that appear in this unit.

- *invalidate a conclusion*
- *refuse consent*
- *pay compensation*

5.1 **Complete each sentence below using one of the verbs in the box. Pay attention to the underlined noun in each sentence and find a verb that collocates with that noun. Use each verb once only.**

demonstrate	be	follow	give	pay	predict
coordinate	justify	make	maximize	meet	

Education

1. All applicants must _____ the entry <u>criteria</u> for this course.

2. They must also _____ a <u>commitment</u> to this highly specialized field of study.

3. Students are expected to _____ an active <u>contribution</u> to the life of the university.

4. The principal has had to _____ his <u>actions</u> after firing a teacher.

5. Universities _____ students hundreds of thousands of pounds each year to <u>compensate</u> for their mistakes.

6. The questions _____ a logical <u>sequence</u>.

Politics

7. The government is going to _____ the relief <u>effort</u> as numerous aid agencies arrive in the affected area.

8. The Ministry of Finance will _____ its <u>consent</u> to the release of more funds to help the victims.

9. With both parties level in the opinion polls, it is very difficult to _____ the <u>outcome</u> of the election.

10. There _____ a big <u>shift</u> in public opinion since the last election.

11. One of the goals of the new government is to _____ <u>results</u> in the health sector.

5.2 **Choose one verb from the box that fits best with all the nouns in each group.**

justify	shift	emphasize	dominate	illustrate	exclude

1. _____ an action, an argument, the cost, a position

2. _____ a point, a need, the importance, the value

3. _____ funds, attention, responsibility, power

4. _____ the world, the market, the industry, the news

5. _____ the point, the difficulty, the problem, the importance

6. _____ people, children, evidence, the possibility

5.3 **Complete the sentences below with an appropriate verb + noun combination from Ex 5.2. The first letter of each noun is given to help you. Pay attention to the form and tense of the verb in each sentence.**

1. _C_____ who are _____ from school often end up wandering the streets.

2. We can _____ this p_____ by showing you a diagram.

3. The report _____ the i_____ of implementing safety standards.

4. Men still tend to _____ the w_____ of professional sport – there are hardly any women involved in football management, for example.

5. The government hopes the latest good news from overseas will _____ the media's a_____ away from the current economic problems.

Adjectives and nouns

Look at these adjective + noun combinations that appear in this unit.
- *full compensation*
- *new vocabulary*
- *active contribution*

5.4   **Match the adjectives on the left with the nouns on the right to make combinations from this unit.**

Adjective		Noun
1. initial	☐	**a.** male
2. ethnic	☐	**b.** reasons
3. positive	☐	**c.** treatment
4. dominant	☐	**d.** compensation
5. particular	☐	**e.** minorities
6. different	☐	**f.** performance
7. alternative	☐	**g.** outcome
8. valid	☐	**h.** components
9. enormous	☐	**i.** shift
10. full	☐	**j.** techniques

5.5   **Use your dictionary to find nouns that can be used in combination with the following adjectives.**

1. initial _____

2. sufficient _____

3. specific _____

4. valid _____

5. reliable _____

6. minor _____

5.6 **Look at the underlined words in the following sentences. Identify different combinations of verbs, nouns, adjectives and prepositions. Then answer the questions that follow.**

Environment

1. The disposal of non-recyclable items can have serious <u>implications</u> for the environment.

2. The council's plan to build a new waste disposal plant was abandoned because of the potential social and environmental <u>implications</u>.

3. The Ministry has proposed a <u>scheme</u> to make more use of wind and tidal energy.

4. Under a new government <u>scheme</u>, householders are being encouraged to switch to solar energy.

5. Voluntary workers make a huge <u>contribution</u> to local environmental projects.

Business

6. Small businesses have made a significant <u>contribution</u> to the economic regeneration of the high street.

7. Payment of the full amount can be delayed under certain <u>circumstances</u>.

8. In exceptional <u>circumstances</u>, a refund may be considered.

9. The purpose of this meeting is to draw up a simple <u>framework</u> with which we can move forward.

10. This proposal provides a <u>framework</u> for future discussion.

11. Most people are willing to allow their names to be used for publicity if this is done with their prior <u>consent</u>.

Health

12. Toxicity is not the only <u>criterion</u> for classifying a drug as dangerous.

13. The government is drawing up new <u>criteria</u> for the classification of drugs and other harmful substances.

14. This disease affects a significant <u>proportion</u> of the population.

15. Although the majority of M.E. sufferers are women, a small <u>proportion</u> – about five per cent – are men.

16. The government's <u>reaction</u> to the bird flu epidemic has been unhelpful.

17. When bird flu broke out, the government's first <u>reaction</u> was to increase the number of staff in hospitals.

18. The heart operation can only be performed with the subject's written <u>consent</u>.

Questions:

a. What verbs are used before these nouns?

<u>draw up, provide</u>　a framework

_____ implications

_____ criteria

_____ a contribution

b. What adjectives are used before these nouns?

_____ implications

_____ circumstances

_____ criterion/criteria

_____ proportion

_____ reaction

_____ consent

_____ contribution

c. What prepositions are used after these nouns?

criterion/criteria _____

framework _____

proportion _____

reaction _____

d. What prepositions are used before these nouns?

_____ circumstances

_____ consent

Task 6	Word grammar

Discovering noun patterns

You studied the following patterns in Unit 5. Ex 6.1 will help you notice these patterns in the academic texts you read.

- noun + preposition, e.g., *alternative to*
- noun followed by *that*, e.g., *implication that*
- noun + noun, e.g., *health aspects*
- noun followed by *to be*, e.g., *the alternative is*

6.1 **Look at the underlined nouns in the sentences below and answer the following questions.**

1. Is a preposition used after the noun? If so, what preposition?

   a. _____ b. _____ c. _____ d. _____ e. _____ f. _____

   g. _____ h. _____ i. _____ j. _____ k. _____ l. _____

   m. _____ n. _____ o. _____

2. Which nouns are followed by *that* + clause?

   _____

3. What prepositions come before *core* and *instances*?

   _____

4. Which noun is followed by *to* + infinitive?

   _____

5. Which nouns are followed by the verb *to be* (i.e., *is*, *are*, etc.) + *to* + infinitive?

   _____

Health

a. Cold Laser treatment is offered as an <u>alternative</u> to invasive surgery.

b. The <u>alternative</u> is to operate on the patient immediately, although this might cause complications.

c. Applications from non-smokers were encouraged, with the <u>implication</u> that smokers would not be considered for the position.

d. This new legislation banning smoking in pubs and restaurants has profound <u>implications</u> for social life in the UK.

e. The research examined the <u>implications</u> of prohibiting smoking in all public places in Ireland and Norway.

f. The legislation lays particular <u>emphasis</u> on the health risks of passive smoking.

g. A significant <u>proportion</u> of young people start smoking in their early teens.

h. Peer pressure is at the <u>core</u> of the problem.

i. Researchers have also come across many <u>instances</u> of health problems relating to poor diet.

Environment

j. The continuing lack of rainfall is having a serious impact on the <u>volume</u> of water in the reservoir.

k. There are various <u>techniques</u> for dealing with industrial pollution.

l. The authorities are examining a number of <u>schemes</u> to pump water into the reservoir from nearby rivers.

m. However, the <u>reaction</u> to these plans has not been positive.

n. Conservationists are calling for alternative <u>techniques</u> of water conservation to be applied in this particular case.

o. In this particular <u>instance</u>, the authorities admit they may have made an error of judgement.

Noun + noun combinations

Here are some more examples of noun + noun combinations from previous exercises in this unit.
- *pie chart*
- *government scheme*

6.2 **Match the nouns on the left with the nouns on the right to make noun + noun combinations from this unit.**

Noun 1

Noun 2

1. construction ☐   a. change

2. ozone ☐   b. project

3. climate ☐   c. layer

4. repair ☐   d. fossils

5. car ☐   e. pressure

6. shellfish ☐   f. work

7. flood ☐   g. infrastructure

8. stock ☐   h. exchange

9. peer ☐   i. engine

10. transport ☐   j. defences

Note: For more information about noun patterns, see Unit 5.

Transitive or intransitive verbs

In earlier exercises in this unit, we have seen examples of the following verbs which show that they can be used with noun phrases as objects: *constrain, coordinate, demonstrate, illustrate, justify, link, shift, invalidate, maximize, emphasize, dominate, exclude.* All of these verbs are transitive.

Example:
- *Children who are excluded from school often end up wandering the streets during the day.*

6.3   The tables below show other verbs from AWL Sublist 3 which are always transitive or always intransitive. Complete the tables below by putting the verbs from the box in the correct column.

correspond	deduce	~~negate~~	~~publish~~
~~fund~~	~~specify~~	ensure	imply
~~remove~~	~~consent~~		interact

Transitive verbs	
fund	specify
negate	
publish	
remove	

Intransitive verbs	
consent	

6.4   **Copy an example sentence from your dictionary for each of the transitive verbs from the completed table in Ex 6.3.**

fund: _Many people believe that the insurgents are being funded from abroad._

_____

_____

_____

_____

_____

_____

_____

_____

_____

_____

_____

_____

6.5   **Copy an example sentence from your dictionary for each of the intransitive verbs from the completed table in Ex 6.3.**

consent: After a long delay, they finally consented to the construction of the

new motorway.

_____

_____

_____

_____

_____

_____

_____

_____

_____

_____

_____

_____

_____

Verbs that are both transitive and intransitive
The following verbs are sometimes transitive and sometimes intransitive: *compensate, contribute, convene, register.*

6.6   **Look at the verbs as they are used in these sentences and decide if they are transitive (VT) or intransitive (VI).**

1.   My parents said they would <u>contribute</u> towards the cost of my driving lessons. (___)

2.   David's enthusiasm <u>compensates</u> for his lack of experience. (___)

3.   The Parliament will next <u>convene</u> on October 4. (___)

4.   Gun owners had until the end of 1990 to <u>register</u> their weapons. (___)

5.   Large retail chains are usually only prepared to <u>locate</u> stores in areas of high population density. (___)

> **Verbs followed by *that* + clause**
>
> In earlier exercises, you will have seen that some verbs can be followed by *that* + clause, for example, in Ex 1.1:
> - *Darwin's observations led him to <u>deduce</u> that animals could adapt to their surroundings.*
>
> and in Ex 2.1:
> - *The data <u>implies</u> that inflation rates might fall next year.*

6.7 **Use your dictionary to check and circle the words in the box that can be used with *that* + clause. Copy example sentences from your dictionary.**

comment	dominate	emphasize	ensure	exclude	demonstrate
illustrate	invalidate	justify	link	maximize	shift

comment: Experts commented that the report was 'full of errors'.

_____

_____

_____

_____

_____

_____

_____

_____

> **Verbs followed by *wh~* + clause**
>
> The following verbs can also be used with a *wh~* word + clause: *illustrate, demonstrate, emphasize, specify.*
> - *The engineer <u>demonstrated</u> how the new equipment worked.*

6.8 **Write sentences by putting the words below in the right order.**

1. we need / illustrate / health care / The two stories / why / better and cheaper

   _____

2. they can do / Good tests / to demonstrate / allow students / what

   _____

3. be delivered / when / specifies / have to / The contract / the machines

   _____

4. work / Regulations / drivers / can / how many hours / specify

_____

5. what / we need / The Prime Minister / to rebuild the economy / emphasized / to do

_____

6. The contract / is not covered / clearly specifies / by the agreement / who

_____

7. believe / The rumours / illustrate / why / tabloid newspapers / about her pregnancy / you should not always

_____

| Task 7 | Review |

It is important you find time to review the exercises you have done in this unit and review what you have learnt.

7.1   Look back through the unit and find:

1. five adjective + noun collocations

_____

_____

2. five noun + noun collocations

_____

_____

3. five nouns often followed by prepositions

_____

_____

4. five words that can be either nouns or verbs

_____

_____

7.2 **Look back over all the exercises you have done and write down phrases that you think are useful and that you want to remember.**

Examples:

… clearly illustrates the point …

… an enormous shift in attitudes …

… has decreased noticeably …

… focusing on research and development …

… make a positive contribution …

… expand rapidly …

… an overgeneralized conclusion …

Make your own notes here.

_____

_____

_____

_____

_____

_____

_____

_____

_____

_____

_____

_____

_____

_____

_____

_____

_____

7.3   **Look at AWL Sublist 3 on pages 172–173. Check the words you don't know in your dictionary and make notes on the meaning and use of the words.**

Example:

Word (word class)	Meaning
consensus (noun)	an opinion that everyone in a group agrees with or accepts

Example phrases:

… a lack of consensus

… consensus that …

… failed to reach a consensus on …

The general consensus was that …

Example sentence:

There is a general consensus among teachers that children should have a broad understanding of the world.

Make your own notes here.

_____

_____

_____

_____

_____

_____

_____

_____

_____

_____

_____

_____

_____

_____

_____

Vocabulary List

Business and Finance
domestic market
economic regeneration
Ministry of Finance
profitability

Environment
Antarctica
conservationist
fossil fuel
harmful substance
industrial pollution
rainfall
reservoir
solar energy
tidal energy
toxicity
waste disposal plant
wind energy

Health
health worker
invasive surgery
medical facility
medical procedure
passive smoking
pharmaceuticals
sufferer

Manufacturing
electrical part
fully guaranteed
goods
manufacturer
repair work

research and
  development
technical specification

Politics
government scheme

Research
public opinion
survey (n)

Science
ape
baboon
biological basis
carbon dating
dominant male
Earth's core
earthquake
fossil
motor behaviour
observation
primate
Richter scale
seed
shellfish
theory of evolution

Society
ethnic minority
peer pressure
population density
voluntary worker

Verbs
abandon
account (for)

adapt
break out
contribute (to)
coordinate
encourage
experience
implement
lay (emphasis on)
lead
predict
prohibit
release
retain
reveal
wander

Other
ancient
applicant
commitment
complication
core
enthusiasm
entry criteria
error of judgement
implication
infrastructure
insurgent
likely cause
logical sequence
loyal
nonetheless
overgeneralized
personnel

phase
prior consent
probable
profound
provocation
publicity
relief effort
remains (n)
responsibility
riot
safety standards
seniority
surroundings
victim
weapon

For web resources relevant to this book, see:
www.englishforacademicstudy.com

This weblink will give you access to help with developing your active scientific vocabulary, with presentations from scientists talking about a variety of topics, as well as lists of high-frequency scientific words and common scientific phrases.

AWL – Sublist 4

In this unit you will:

- familiarize yourself with the word families in AWL Sublist 4
- practise understanding and using these words in context

Task 1   Meanings of words

As you do these exercises, pay special attention to the word class of each individual word.

1.1 **Study the underlined words in the extracts below and think about their meaning.**

Switzerland is a good example of a country where different forms of transport have been fully <u>integrated</u>. A transport strategy has been <u>implemented</u> which fully coordinates timetables for different forms of transport. For example, buses are timetabled to meet arriving trains, and <u>subsequent</u> waiting times are kept to a minimum. The country has adopted an <u>overall</u> strategy for transport, and other forms of transport such as boat services and funicular railways are also included.

Excessive pollution in some urban areas has been <u>attributed</u> to emissions from diesel and petrol engines, and it is <u>apparent</u> that the use of private cars has increased rapidly over the past 30 years. Air pollution is reaching unprecedented levels in some areas, <u>hence</u> the need for urgent measures to limit it. Some local authorities would like to <u>impose</u> strict limits on the use of cars. They feel that the measures currently in force are simply not <u>adequate</u>. They already have considerable powers to deal with traffic problems. For example, in some towns and cities, illegally parked cars may be removed without <u>prior</u> notice.

1.2 **Match the words from Ex 1.1 with the definitions on the right.**

Word		Meaning
1. integrate	☐	**a.** obvious or easy to notice
2. implement	☐	**b.** to force people to accept something
3. subsequent	☐	**c.** for this reason or as a result of this
4. overall	☐	**d.** good enough or sufficient for a specific purpose
5. attribute	☐	**e.** when two or more suitable things are connected to work together more effectively than before
6. apparent	☐	**f.** including everything or considering something as a whole
7. hence	☐	**g.** to believe that a situation or event is caused by something
8. impose	☐	**h.** to make something happen that has been officially decided
9. adequate	☐	**i.** happening previous to a particular time
10. prior	☐	**j.** following on from or coming after something else

1.3 **Complete the pairs of sentences below with the words from Ex 1.2. In each pair, you need the same word for both sentences. In the case of verbs, pay attention to the ending required, e.g., ~s, ~ed, ~ing. In the case of nouns, you may have to decide whether the singular or plural form is appropriate.**

Health

1. The _____ spread of the disease to other regions of the country suggested that it was more virulent than first thought.

    After patients have been vaccinated, the _____ side effects may be unpleasant in some cases.

2. James _____ his long life to the fact that he has never smoked and hasn't touched alcohol for more than 60 years.

    Tom's emotional problems can be _____ to his difficult childhood.

3. The hospital is planning to _____ a ban on eating and drinking on the premises.

    The clinic has _____ a fine for missed appointments.

Business

4. Distribution costs are a major factor, _____ the location of the distribution centre is an important consideration.

   Overseas sales are growing rapidly, _____ the need for a second distribution centre.

5. We were not asked to provide specific details, but simply the _____ picture.

   Having listened to our presentation, they seemed happy with the _____ approach we had taken.

6. The office is quite small, but it's perfectly _____ for two people.

   Unfortunately, we were not given _____ training in how to use the software.

Transport

7. Illegally parked cars may be removed without _____ notice.

   Flights are often cancelled without _____ warning due to adverse weather conditions.

8. It soon became _____ that there was a serious problem with the onboard equipment.

   The flight was cancelled for no _____ reason.

9. The new government should _____ energy policy with transport planning.

   Urban transportation can easily be _____ with national rail systems.

10. Recent attempts to _____ changes within the railway system have met with strong opposition.

    Virgin Trains has decided that the committee's recommendations will be _____ in full.

| Task 2 | **Multi-meaning words** |

2.1 **The underlined words in the sentences below have at least two meanings. Look at how they are used and choose the correct meaning.**

Education

1. The course places particular <u>stress</u> on the need for individual research projects.
   a. a feeling of pressure about your work or social life that can stop you relaxing
   b. force or pressure applied to an object that can break it or make it change its shape
   c. special emphasis given to something

2. Students have to take a <u>series</u> of tests before being enrolled at the college.
   a. a succession of things that happen one after the other but are not necessarily connected
   b. a television or radio programme that appears in sequential parts
   c. a run of matches that two teams play against each other over a period of time

3. The <u>dimensions</u> of the classroom vary considerably.
   a. a factor in a situation (synonym = aspect)
   b. the measurements, for example the length, height and width of something

4. The school imposes a strict dress <u>code</u>.
   a. a system of rules and regulations that dictate people's behaviour
   b. a system where words and numbers are substituted with others to enable people to send secret messages
   c. a number that comes at the beginning of a telephone number to show the receiver's area

5. Almost half the time some teachers spend at school is <u>occupied</u> with paperwork.
   a. something you are thinking about all the time
   b. to be busy doing something
   c. to be using a building or area of land

Politics

6. The military <u>regime</u> is highly unpopular, and there are signs it is losing its grip on power.
   a. a government that is in power in a country, often unelected and ruling in a strict way
   b. a special exercise and dietary plan that is intended to improve your health
   c. a rule structure that controls a particular area of life

7. The prime minister was allowed access to top-secret military bases because of his high security <u>status</u>.
   a. the social or professional rank of a person, when compared with other people
   b. the legal position of an entity
   c. a situation at a particular time, usually in a discussion or argument

8. The new government <u>promotes</u> education and is planning to build new schools throughout the country.
   a. to support something to further its progress
   b. to advance someone to a preferable, more responsible job within an organization
   c. to encourage people to support or use something

9. The <u>output</u> of petrol has increased considerably since the new government came into power.
   a. the quantity of something that can be produced by a person, machine or organization
   b. the data displayed on a computer screen or printed onto paper from it
   c. the volume of electricity or power a piece of equipment can produce

10. Elections are the usual <u>mechanism</u> by which political parties come into power.
    a. an assembly of mechanical items
    b. a way of addressing a problem or getting something done
    c. a structure or behaviour that enables a person to deal with a difficult situation

Task 3   Word classes

3.1   **Use your dictionary to check these words. Then complete the tables with the word class they belong to, i.e., noun, verb, adjective or adverb. Some words belong in more than one class.**

Word	Word class
stress	*verb, noun*
grant	
hypothesis	
civil	
contrast	
cycle	

Word	Word class
internal	
resolve	
principal	
access	
label	
phase	

3.2   **Decide what word class would fill each gap in the following sentences. Write *v*, *n* or *adj* in the brackets after each gap.**

Social Science

1.   Some believe there is a _____ (___) of violence where children who are abused grow up to be abusers.

2.   The idea that there is a link between climate and life expectancy is an interesting _____ (___).

3.   In certain urban areas of Scotland, alcohol and smoking are the _____ (___) causes of disease in adult males.

4.   Although many people have _____ (___) to expert advice on healthy eating habits, few people take advantage of this opportunity.

5.   Health experts have _____ (___) the need to get the message across more clearly.

6.   They see education as the first _____ (___) in the battle to improve public health in this region.

7.   It is interesting to _____ (___) diet and lifestyle in different areas of the country.

8.   But some experts believe that problems related to alcohol and smoking will be extremely difficult to _____ (___).

9. Children who are _____ (___) as 'difficult' may get less attention from teachers.

10. Children under 16 are _____ (___) free dental care.

11. The problem is an _____ (___) matter and will be resolved within the social services department.

12. Claims for financial compensation can be lodged with the _____ (___) courts.

3.3 **Complete the sentences in Ex 3.2 with words from Ex 3.1. In the case of verbs, pay attention to the ending required, e.g., ~s, ~ed, ~ing. In the case of nouns, you may have to decide whether the singular or plural form is appropriate.**

| Task 4 | Word families |

Look at these two sentences.

> We might want to use our knowledge that four feet is the average height in this child's class to <u>predict</u> the average height in another class.

> The two chief concerns of statistics are with (1) <u>summarizing</u> our experience so that we and other people can understand its essential features, and (2) using the <u>summary</u> to make estimates or <u>predictions</u> about what is likely to be the case in other (perhaps future) situations.

Source: Rowntree, D. (1981). *Statistics without Tears: A Primer for Non-Mathematicians*. London: Penguin.

The underlined words, *predict* and *prediction*, come from the same word family, as do the words *summary* and *summarizing*. As we have seen in previous units, this use of members of the same word family helps the author make the writing more cohesive.

Note: For more information on word families, refer back to Unit 3.

4.1 **Complete the table on page 121 with the words from the box. There may be some columns where there are two entries. You may know some other words to complete the light green cells.**

accessible	annually	concentration	promotion
debatable	apparently	occupation	predictable	occupational
statistically	optional	investigation	predictably

Nouns	Verbs	Adjectives	Adverbs
	concentrate		
		annual	
	promote		
debate			
	predict		
statistics			
	investigate		
	occupy		
option			
		apparent	
access			

4.2 **Choose the correct form of the word in brackets to complete the following sentences. In the case of verbs, a different ending may be needed for the word, e.g., ~s, ~ed, ~ing. In the case of nouns, you may have to decide whether the singular or plural form is appropriate.**

Transport

1. Two aeroplanes passed within 100 metres of each other above London. The authorities are carrying out a full _____ into the incident. (investigate)

2. According to _____, you are far less likely to die in a plane crash than in any other regular means of transport. (statistics)

3. The long-term effects of the rapid increase in low-cost airlines are not _____ at this stage. (predict)

4. The rise of budget airlines in Europe has meant that cheap air travel is now _____ to almost everyone in the European Union. (access)

5. High _____ of pollutants have been found around some airports. (concentrate)

Study tip

The two main varieties of American English and British English are very similar. With increased globalization, some of the contrasts are disappearing, e.g., *aeroplane* is increasingly being replaced in British English by the American *airplane*.

Business and Finance

6. The survey found a sharp fall in the number of people in manual _____. (occupy)

7. It also found that young males were more interested in high pay and _____ than older people, and less worried about job security. (promote)

8. People with no academic qualifications often have no _____ but to take low-paid, unattractive work. (option)

9. It is _____ whether an economy based on service industries can provide long-term stability in employment. (debate)

10. The factory closed five years ago, but, _____, the effects on the local community are still being felt. (predict)

11. _____, the potential effects of the closure were not taken into consideration at the time. (apparent)

4.3 **Choose the correct forms of the word in brackets to complete the sentences.**

1. Scientists have been _investigating_ the causes of global warming. Their _investigations_ have reached a number of different conclusions. (investigate)

2. Early in 2006, Parliament _____ the introduction of identity cards. The _____ was often inconclusive. Finally a compromise was reached. (debate)

3. The entrance to the museum has been widened to improve _____ for disabled people. However, many of the other public buildings in the city are still not fully _____ to people in wheelchairs. (access)

4. During the Second World War, the Germans _____ France. Many French people consider the _____ to be the most painful period in French history. (occupy)

5. Some scientists _____ that the Earth's temperature will rise by as much as 5°C over the next 20 years. Other scientists dispute these _____, however. (predict)

6. The _____ into the cause of the crash is continuing. The _____ say it could take several weeks to complete. (investigate)

7. Good _____ skills are essential in the modern world, but many employers have found that school leavers are relatively poor _____. (communicate)

Prefixes

The following prefixes are used with a number of the words from AWL Sublist 4.

Prefix	Meaning
re~	again
in~, un~	not, the opposite of

4.4 **Which of the above prefixes can be used with the following words?**

1. accessible _____

2. adequate _____

3. communicative _____

4. cycle _____

5. resolved _____

6. predictable _____

4.5 **Complete the following sentences using either:**
- the correct form of the word in brackets; or
- a prefix + the correct form of the word in brackets

In the case of verbs, pay attention to the ending required, e.g., ~ed, ~ing, ~s.

Environment

1. Unfortunately there is _____ provision for the recycling of waste in this area. (adequate)

2. Countries like Canada are planning to _____ almost 100 per cent of their waste. (cycle)

3. Local authorities must provide _____ waste disposal facilities. (accessible)

4. If we continue to produce waste at the current rate, we are facing an _____ future. (predictable)

5. Problems with the disposal of non-recyclable items such as batteries remain _____. (resolved)

6. One of the main difficulties we face is that the person charged with selling the idea of recycling to the public is an unresponsive and _____ individual. (communicative)

Task 5	Collocations

Verbs and nouns

Look at these verb + noun combinations that appear in this unit.
- *impose limits*
- *promote education*

5.1 Choose one noun from the box that fits best with each verb to make a combination from this unit. Some verbs should be combined with more than one noun.

a strategy	a ban	the need	the causes
limits	no option	a fine	access
~~France~~	recommendations	permission	an investigation

1. occupy   <u>France</u>

2. grant   _____

3. implement   _____

4. impose   _____

5. give   _____

6. stress   _____

7. carry out   _____

8. have   _____

9. investigate   _____

5.2 Choose one verb from the box that fits best with all the nouns in each group.

commit	predict	~~promote~~	retain	stress	undertake

1. <u>promote</u>   development, growth, awareness, health

2. _____   the outcome, the future, the weather, rain, growth

3. _____   independence, staff, control, heat

4. _____   a crime, a robbery, an offence, suicide

5. _____   the need, the importance, the urgency, the value

6. _____   an action, an analysis, a project, a task

5.3   **Complete the sentences below with an appropriate verb + noun combination from Ex 5.2. The first letter of each noun is given to help you. Pay attention to the form and tense of the verb in each sentence.**

1. The use of fertilizer _____ plant g_____.

2. The government intends to _____ c_____ over the security forces.

3. Nutritionists _____ the i_____ of a balanced diet.

4. Dr Johnson _____ the enormous t_____ of compiling the first comprehensive English dictionary.

5. Men _____ far more violent c_____ than women.

6. Economists are _____ very low g_____ for the first quarter of the next financial year.

Adjectives and nouns

Look at these adjective + noun combinations that appear in this unit.
- *main difficulties*
- *unattractive work*

5.4   **Match the adjectives on the left with the nouns on the right to make combinations from this unit.**

Adjective		Noun
1. subsequent	☐	a. notice
2. prior	☐	b. provision
3. emotional	☐	c. concern
4. inadequate	☐	d. problems
5. overall	☐	e. strategy
6. chief	☐	f. waiting times

5.5   **Use your dictionary to find nouns that can be used in combination with the following adjectives.**

1. statistical   _____

2. emerging   _____

3. overall   _____

4. internal   _____

5. adequate   _____

6. domestic   _____

7. prior   _____

8. civil   _____

9. hypothetical   _____

10. principal   _____

5.6   **Look at the underlined words in the following sentences. Identify different combinations of verbs, nouns, adjectives and prepositions. Then answer the questions on page 127.**

1. <u>Statistics</u> show that the number of people voting in local elections is falling steadily.

2. The findings confirmed the <u>hypothesis</u> that smokers are at greater risk of heart attack than non-smokers.

3. The new government is planning to reform the justice system in order to break the <u>cycle</u> of crime and reoffending.

4. It's too early to make any <u>predictions</u> about the make-up of the next government.

5. This task requires a peaceful environment and total <u>concentration</u>.

6. Stockbrokers need direct <u>access</u> to the latest financial data.

7. We place particular <u>stress</u> on first-class customer service.

8. It was discovered that the forensic scientist had committed a serious <u>error</u>.

9. These documents have no legal <u>status</u> in Britain.

10. The government is hoping to achieve their <u>goal</u> of providing a computer for every classroom.

11. What other <u>options</u> do we have?

Question:

What verbs are used with these nouns (either before or after)?

a. stress   _place_____

b. access   _____

c. hypothesis   _____

d. statistics   _____

e. predictions   _____

f. concentration   _____

g. error   _____

h. cycle   _____

i. status   _____

j. options   _____

k. goals   _____

5.7 **Look at the underlined words in the following sentences. Identify different combinations of verbs, nouns, adjectives and prepositions. Then answer the questions that follow.**

Business

1. Statistical data can be used to make realistic economic <u>predictions</u>.

2. The book makes economics easily <u>accessible</u> to the general reader.

3. A number of people in the company are under a lot of <u>stress</u> right now and have little time to relax.

4. The new products are aggressively <u>promoted</u> and marketed.

5. This approach <u>contrasts</u> sharply with the methods used by the previous marketing manager.

6. The objective is to adjust the results so that the <u>error</u> in the statistics is minimized.

7. The project is still in the experimental <u>phase</u> and the outcome will determine the company's decision.

8. Over the years, bankers have acquired high social <u>status</u>.

Education

9. According to official <u>statistics</u>, girls achieve considerably higher grades at primary school level than boys.

10. The latest <u>prediction</u> is that, due to the recent increase in fees, the number of British students at university will fall considerably.

11. Students embarking on degree courses need to be able to <u>communicate</u> effectively in both speech and writing.

12. The college has a high <u>concentration</u> of international students.

13. The school has adopted a fully <u>integrated</u> approach to supporting dyslexic students.

14. Students experiencing emotional <u>stress</u> are advised to see the university counsellor.

15. Students must have definite <u>goals</u> towards which they can work.

Questions:

a. What adjectives are used before these nouns?

_____ statistics

_____ phase

_____ concentration

_____ stress

_____ prediction(s)

_____ status

_____ goals

b. What prepositions are used before these nouns?

_____ statistics

_____ stress

_____ phase

c. What adverbs are used with these words (either before or after)?

integrated _____

promoted _____

accessible _____

communicate _____

contrasts _____

| Task 6 | **Word grammar** |

Discovering noun patterns

You studied the following patterns in Unit 5. Ex 6.1 will help you notice these patterns in the texts you read.
- noun + preposition, e.g., *attitudes towards*
- noun followed by *that*, e.g., *hypothesis that*
- noun followed by *to* + infinitive, e.g., *commitment to reduce*

6.1 **Look at the underlined words in the sentences on page 130 and answer the following questions.**

1. Is a preposition used to connect the underlined word to the following noun? If so, what preposition?

   a. _____ b. _____ c. _____ d. _____ e. _____ f. _____

   g. _____ h. _____ i. _____ j. _____ k. _____ l. _____

   m. _____ n. _____ o. _____ p. _____ q. _____ r. _____

2. Which nouns are followed by *that* + clause (or *is/are* + *that* clause)?

   _____

3. Which noun is followed by a preposition + *wh~* word + clause?

   _____

4. What preposition comes before *contrast*?

   _____

5. Which nouns are followed by *to* + infinitive?

   _____

6. Which underlined word is not a noun? What word class is it and what comes after this word?

   _____

Education

a. It's the teacher's <u>job</u>* to ensure that students are well prepared for the exam.

b. The college has introduced new policies in order to change <u>attitudes</u> towards multiculturalism.

c. Many people take the <u>attitude</u> that mature students should be working rather studying.

d. There is clearly an <u>error</u> in the published exam results.

e. The decision to reduce teaching staff was an <u>error</u> of judgement.

f. The university has several <u>mechanisms</u> for settling disputes.

g. Students usually have no <u>option</u> but to live in rented accommodation.

h. Susan attended class <u>despite</u> the fact that she had a high temperature.

i. <u>Despite</u> their hard work, a great number of students failed their exam.

Job in this situation means 'a specific responsibility'.

Social Science

j. The latest <u>prediction</u> is that 80 per cent of households will have a PC within five years.

k. <u>Predictions</u> of violence in the run-up to the elections are growing.

l. There was a lot of <u>debate</u> about whether the elections should go ahead as planned.

m. The government has made a <u>commitment</u> to reduce traffic congestion in major cities.

n. They say they have a strong <u>commitment</u> to cheap and efficient public transport.

o. The <u>contrast</u> between the north and the south of the country is very evident.

p. Unemployment is still rising in the north, in <u>contrast</u> to the south, where it is falling steadily.

q. Experts believe that the <u>cycle</u> of violence in domestic abuse is extremely difficult to break.

r. The findings support the <u>hypothesis</u> that there is a link between social background and academic failure.

Noun + noun combinations

Here are some more examples of noun + noun combinations from previous exercises in this unit.

- *transport strategy*
- *diesel engine*
- *air pollution*

6.2   **Match the nouns on the left with the nouns on the right to make noun + noun combinations from this unit.**

Noun 1   **Noun 2**

1. energy   ☐   a. conditions

2. life   ☐   b. sentence

3. distribution   ☐   c. regime

4. prison   ☐   d. costs

5. weather   ☐   e. expectancy

6. research   ☐   f. policy

7. military   ☐   g. project

6.3   **Use your dictionary to find nouns that can be used in combination with the following nouns (either before or after).**

1. code   _____

2. error   _____

3. project   _____

4. mechanism   _____

Note: For more information about noun patterns, see Unit 4.

Adjectives + clauses or verb phrases
We have already seen in this and previous units that both verbs and nouns can be followed by clauses. Some adjectives can also be followed by (*that*) + clause or by a phrase. **Examples:** ■ We are <u>confident that</u> the stadium will be finished in time. ■ It's <u>normal to feel</u> nervous before visiting the dentist. ■ It's <u>worth</u> talking to your tutor before making a final decision.

6.4 **Look at the following sentences and notice particularly the way the underlined adjectives are connected to what follows them. Then answer the questions that follow.**

Crime and the Law

1. Funds have been made <u>available</u> to assist the police in fighting cybercrime.

2. It is more <u>economical</u> to give an offender community service than a prison sentence.

3. It was <u>evident</u> that he was involved in the attack.

4. It is <u>illegal</u> for anyone in this country to possess or sell narcotics.

5. It is highly <u>significant</u> that many of these crimes are committed by drug users.

6. The amount is not <u>sufficient</u> to cover all the legal costs.

7. It is <u>apparent</u> that we have a major problem with alcohol-related crimes.

Culture

8. It would not be <u>appropriate</u> for me to judge his religious beliefs.

9. It seems <u>appropriate</u> that we should follow their customs when visiting their country.

10. The tourists thought it was <u>abnormal</u> for such a young child to be carrying a weapon.

11. Tina is absolutely <u>positive</u> that travelling will broaden her understanding of other cultures.

12. It is <u>traditional</u> to eat fish on Good Friday.

13. It may be <u>valid</u> to say that his attitude towards ethnic diversity may be interpreted as racism.

14. It is <u>debatable</u> whether there should be a ban on burqas in British universities.

15. It seems <u>obvious</u> that customs and traditions should be respected.

16. It is fairly <u>predictable</u> that the cultural differences between them will create some misunderstandings.

Note: The phrase … *for someone* … can be added to most of these adjectives, with the possible exception of *valid*. It is also possible to drop it altogether, e.g., *It is illegal to develop biological weapons.*

Questions

a. Which adjectives are used with *that* + clause?

_____

b. Which adjectives are used with *for* (*someone*) + *to* + infinitive?

_____

c. Which adjectives are used with *to* + infinitive?

_____

d. What is different about the pattern used after *debatable*?

_____

Transitive or intransitive verbs

In earlier exercises in this unit, we have seen examples of the following verbs which show that they can be used with noun phrases as objects: *attribute, commit, grant, implement, impose, integrate, label, occupy, predict, promote, resolve, retain, stress, undertake.*

Examples:

- *Different forms of transport have been fully <u>integrated</u>.*
- *Excessive pollution has been <u>attributed</u> to emissions from petrol and diesel engines.*
- *Children who are <u>labelled</u> 'difficult' may get less attention from teachers.*

Notice that in these examples, the three verbs are used passively. All transitive verbs can be used passively.

6.5 **Here are some other example sentences. Indicate whether the verbs are used in the passive or active form.**

1. Some local authorities would like to <u>impose</u> strict limits on the use of cars. <u>active</u>

2. A transport strategy has been <u>implemented</u> which fully coordinates timetables for different forms of transport. _____

3. Regular exercise <u>promotes</u> good health and normal sleep patterns. _____

4. Almost half the time teachers spend at school is <u>occupied</u> with paperwork. _____

5. The US plans to <u>retain</u> control over the security forces. _____

6.6 **Complete the tables below by putting the verbs from the box in the correct column.**

access   domesticate   emerge   implicate   internalize

Transitive verbs	Intransitive verbs

6.7 **Copy an example sentence from your dictionary for each of the transitive verbs from the completed table in Ex 6.6.**

_____

_____

_____

_____

_____

_____

_____

6.8 **Copy an example sentence from your dictionary for each of the intransitive verbs from the completed table in Ex 6.6.**

_____

_____

_____

_____

_____

_____

_____

Verbs that are both transitive and intransitive

The following verbs are sometimes transitive and sometimes intransitive: _commit, communicate, concentrate, confer, contrast, resolve, project, summarize._

6.9　**Look at the verbs as they are used in these sentences and decide if they are transitive (VT) or intransitive (VI).**

Language and Linguistics

1. German speakers are <u>concentrated</u> mainly in the northeast of Italy. (___)

2. The report <u>concentrated</u> on bilingual education. (___)

3. Although English is the national language, the majority of people <u>communicate</u> with each other in Spanish. (___)

4. The information was verbally <u>communicated</u>. (___)

5. Table 4.7 <u>summarizes</u> the connection between language acquisition and age. (___)

Environment

6. To <u>summarize</u>, in most cases yields were higher in years with higher rainfall. (___)

7. The relatively small amount of waste recycled in Britain <u>contrasts</u> sharply with that of Canada and Switzerland. (___)

8. The study <u>contrasts</u> the levels of carbon dioxide in the Earth's atmosphere in 1950 with the levels present today. (___)

9. Officials are <u>projecting</u> a ten per cent increase in the amount of glass recycled over the next five years. (___)

10. The jetty <u>projects</u> more than 400 metres into the sea and creates an artificial reef. (___)

11. After the earthquake, the authorities <u>resolved</u> to rebuild the city. (___)

12. The issue of toxic waste disposal by the factory has finally been <u>resolved</u>. (___)

Verbs followed by *that* + clause
In earlier exercises, you will have seen that some verbs can be followed by *that* + clause, for example, in Ex 4.3: ■ *Some scientists <u>predict that</u> the Earth's temperature will rise by as much as 5°C over the next 20 years.* and in Ex 3.2: ■ *But some experts <u>believe that</u> problems related to alcohol and smoking will be extremely difficult to resolve.*

6.10 Use your dictionary to check and circle the words in the box that can be used with *that* + clause. Copy example sentences from your dictionary.

communicate	debate	emerge	hypothesize
(predict)	project	resolve	stress

predict: Industry experts predict that another 600 pubs will close by the end of the year.

Verbs followed by *wh~* word + clause

Only two verbs from AWL Sublist 4 can be followed by *wh~* word + clause: *predict*, *debate*.

Example:

- Ministers *have been debating whether* to raise taxes.

6.11 Use your dictionary to find other example sentences with *predict* and *debate* and *wh~* word + clause.

Task 7   Review

It is important you find time to review the exercises you have done in this unit and review what you have learnt.

7.1 **Look back through the unit and find:**

1. five adjective + noun collocations

---

2. five noun + noun collocations

_____

_____

3. five nouns often followed by prepositions

_____

_____

4. five words that can be either nouns or verbs

_____

_____

7.2 **Look back over all the exercises you have done and write down phrases that you think are useful and that you want to remember.**

Examples:

… to impose strict limits on …

… the measures currently in force …

… few people take advantage of this opportunity …

… were not taken into consideration …

… in the experimental phase …

… easily accessible to …

… despite the fact that …

… support this hypothesis …

Make your own notes here.

_____

_____

_____

_____

_____

_____

_____

_____

7.3 **Look at AWL Sublist 4 on pages 174–175. Check the words you don't know in your dictionary and make notes on the meanings and use of the words.**

Example:

Word (word class)	Meaning
ethnic (*adj*)	relating to a particular race, nation or tribe and its customs and traditions

Example phrases:

ethnic groups, ethnic background, ethnic divisions, ethnic cooking, ethnic cleansing

Make your own notes here.

_____

_____

_____

_____

_____

_____

_____

_____

_____

_____

_____

_____

_____

_____

_____

_____

_____

_____

Vocabulary List

Business and Finance
budget airline
customer service
distribution centre
distribution costs
economist
financial year
stockbroker

Education
academic qualification
bilingual education
degree course
school leaver

Environment
air pollution
condition
disposal
energy policy
fertilizer
non-recyclable items
pollutant
recycling

Health
balanced diet
fatal disease
heart attack
life expectancy
lifestyle
narcotics
nutritionist
regular exercise
sleep pattern
virulent

Crime and the Law
claim (n)
dispute (n)
evidence
financial compensation
imprisonment
legal position

legal status
offence
prison sentence
robbery

Politics
committee
local election
military regime

Science
experimental phase
forensic scientist
life cycle

Society
ethnic background
ethnic cleansing
ethnic division
ethnic group
identity card
local community
social services
urban area

Verbs
commit
divorce
embark
implicate
link
lodge
minimize
recycle
retain
stress
take (into
   consideration)
undertake
vaccinate

Other
abnormal
analysis
awareness

ban (n)
biological weapon
closure
comprehensive
compromise (n)
consideration
emotional problem
excessive
expert advice
facilities
fully integrated
Good Friday
grip (n)
in full
incident
inconclusive
job security
long-term effects
make-up
manual occupation
paperwork
period (of time)
permission
prior notice
provision
recommendation
run-up
security forces
social status
stability
suicide
traditional
traffic congestion
unelected
unpleasant
unprecedented
unresponsive
urban
urgency
violent

For web resources relevant to this book, see:
www.englishforacademicstudy.com

These weblinks will give you access to news stories, magazine articles, trivia and cartoons, with definitions of all words available at the click of a mouse, as well as games and quizzes to test your knowledge of academic vocabulary.

AWL – Sublist 5

In this unit you will:

- familiarize yourself with the word families in AWL Sublist 5
- practise understanding and using these words in context

| Task 1 | Meanings of words |

1.1 **Study the underlined words in the extracts below and think about their meaning.**

Environment

1. People are becoming increasingly <u>aware</u> of the potential damage to the environment caused by the rapid increase in budget air travel.

2. Reducing carbon emissions is a <u>challenge</u> faced by all governments in the modern era.

3. Many activists are calling on governments to <u>enforce</u> laws governing environmental damage more stringently.

4. Switching to non-fossil fuel <u>substitutes</u> could cost billions, but the long-term benefits are considerable.

5. Reducing the amount of fossil fuels being burnt is one of the <u>fundamental</u> tasks governments will face in the coming decade.

Travel

6. If present <u>trends</u> continue, the number of airline passengers is expected to increase by 60 per cent in the next ten years.

7. Cheap air travel for all has become a <u>symbol</u> of the first decade of the 21st century.

8. Experts are becoming increasingly concerned about the <u>welfare</u> of passengers who travel frequently on long-haul flights.

9. Analysts believe a tax on aviation fuel would bring in a large amount of <u>revenue</u> for the government.

10. Others argue that people will have to <u>modify</u> their travel habits, taking more holidays at home and using other 'greener' forms of transport.

Business and Finance

11. The company structure does not <u>facilitate</u> efficient work flow.

12. Exchange-rate <u>stability</u> depends on a number of factors, including inflation and bank lending rates.

13. Making the <u>transition</u> to a market economy has proved difficult for some of the former Soviet states.

14. The <u>ratio</u> of employees to managerial staff is only 5:1 in some organizations.

1.2   **Match the words from Ex 1.1 with the definitions on the right.**

Word		Meaning
1. aware	☐	**a.** a person or thing that is thought of as representing a bigger idea
2. challenge	☐	**b.** the state of staying balanced and not altering
3. enforce	☐	**c.** to allow something to happen in an easier way
4. substitute	☐	**d.** to ensure someone abides by something
5. fundamental	☐	**e.** something that is used instead of the thing that you normally use, because the usual thing is not available
6. trend	☐	**f.** to know of something's existence
7. symbol	☐	**g.** the health and happiness of a person
8. welfare	☐	**h.** something which tests a person's energy and determination
9. revenue	☐	**i.** the change from one form or state to another
10. modify	☐	**j.** the monetary gain that a business organization receives, often from sales
11. facilitate	☐	**k.** a subtle change or development that seems likely to continue
12. stability	☐	**l.** to make small changes to something to increase its effectiveness
13. transition	☐	**m.** how two things relate to each other as numbers
14. ratio	☐	**n.** the most essential and simple part of something

1.3   **Complete the pairs of sentences below with words from Ex 1.2. In each pair, you need the same word for both sentences. In the case of verbs, pay attention to the ending required, e.g., ~s, ~ed, ~ing. In the case of nouns, you have to decide whether the singular or plural form is appropriate.**

1.   Warm clothing is _____ to survival in the mountains.

Attitudes need to _____ change if areas of outstanding natural beauty are to be preserved.

2. The strike is believed to have cost the newspaper over £10 million in lost _____.

To make matters worse, it has also lost a lot of advertising _____ as a result of the dispute.

3. Mountain rangers should be _____ of the dangers a sudden change in air pressure can cause.

Tim suddenly became _____ of someone following him.

4. Driving a car all day is no _____ for healthy exercise.

Vegetarian mince can be _____ as a healthy alternative to beef.

5. After the doctors had treated the infection, the patient's condition became _____.

The first task of the new government will be to make the economy _____.

6. The government says it is not responsible for the _____ of its citizens while they are abroad.

This company takes great care to safeguard the _____ of its workforce at all times.

7. After 15 years in the same job, I need a new _____.

The problem of global warming is hugely _____ for leaders of the developed world.

8. Researchers have noticed _____ that indicate people are spending an increasing amount of money on leisure travel.

A growing _____ in British society is for young people to borrow money to buy property.

9. Nobody _____ the rules in the manager's absence.

Parking regulations will be strictly _____.

10. The seating plan in this aircraft can be _____ to increase or reduce the number of seats available.

The manufacturer will _____ the engine so that the plane gives a better performance.

11. The new terminal has greatly _____ travel to and from the capital.

A relaxed and open-minded approach can _____ language learning.

12. The cross is generally regarded as one of the principal _____ of the Christian religion.

   In the new democracies of Eastern Europe, anything that represented a _____ of the former communist regimes was quickly removed.

13. The _____ from a communist system to a free-market economy proved to be difficult in many of the former Soviet states.

   She found it particularly difficult to make the _____ from school to university.

14. The _____ of teachers to pupils in some British primary schools can be as high as 1:35.

   The _____ of men to women in the nursing profession is around 1:25.

Task 2	Multi-meaning words

2.1 **The underlined words in the sentences below have at least two meanings. Look at how they are used and choose the correct meaning.**

Business

1. The sales <u>targets</u> for next year have been reduced following this year's poor performance.
   a. something that you are trying to achieve
   b. something you try to hit in a sport or a game
   c. something you plan to attack

2. Many companies today are operating on extremely tight <u>margins</u>.
   a. the column of space down the side of a page
   b. the difference in the number of points between the winners and the losers of a sports event or competition
   c. the difference between what it costs to buy or produce something and its selling price

3. The board has questioned Robert's <u>capacity</u> to manage such a large number of people.
   a. the amount of something that can be put in a receptacle
   b. one's ability to do something
   c. the maximum amount of goods that an organization can produce

4. A new business <u>compound</u> for offices and businesses is currently under construction.
   a. a substance found predominantly in chemistry which contains atoms from two or more elements
   b. an enclosed area that contains a group of buildings
   c. a combination of two or more nouns or adjectives, used as a single word

Science and Technology

5. The software is available in different <u>versions</u> for different types of computer.
    a. a variation of an original
    b. a person's description of an event or thing, which may be different from the description given by another person
    c. a way of explaining something that is typical of a particular group, e.g., 'the Marxist version of history'

6. Access to the <u>network</u> and Internet access is restricted to students holding a membership card.
    a. a system of lines, wires, roads, etc., that join up with each other and are interconnected
    b. a set of computers that are connected to each other so that information can pass between them
    c. people or organizations, etc., that are connected to each other or that work together as a group

7. It became apparent that the problem with the computer was that the <u>monitor</u> wasn't working.
    a. a computer screen
    b. a piece of equipment that measures and records data
    c. a person whose job is to watch an activity or a situation to see how it changes or develops

8. The first <u>generation</u> of mobile phones suffered from being extremely bulky and heavy compared with the ones in use today.
    a. the people in society who are of the same or a similar age
    b. a set of items that were developed at a similar time
    c. the system of production involved in making something

Current Affairs

9. The <u>prime</u> cause of Kuwait's political crisis appeared to be corruption.
    a. most important; main
    b. of premium quality
    c. stands out as being the most appropriate for a specific purpose

> **Study tip**
>
> Some words have very different meanings depending on their word class, e.g., *objective, prime* and *monitor.*

10. Johannesburg is working hard to clean up its <u>image</u>.
    a. the general belief that people tend to have of someone or something
    b. what comes into your mind when you think about someone or something
    c. the reflection you see when you look in a mirror

11. Depending on your personal <u>perspective</u>, the group are either terrorists or freedom fighters.
    a. a particular person's approach to thinking about something
    b. to consider something from many angles to decide on its relevance or accuracy
    c. the art of representation of distance as the eye sees it

12. The <u>conflict</u> in the south of the country shows little sign of dying down.
    a. where two or more people or groups don't agree or argue about something
    b. heavy fighting or even war between countries or groups
    c. a situation in which two or more different needs or influences coexist with difficulty

Task 3   Word classes

3.1 **Check these words in a dictionary. Then complete the tables with the word class they belong to, i.e., noun, verb, adjective or adverb. Some words belong in more than one class.**

Word	Word class
prime	*noun, verb, adjective*
conflict	
decline	
challenge	
contact	
compound	

Word	Word class
monitor	
network	
reject	
objective	
target	
alternate	

3.2 **Decide what word class would fill each gap in the following sentences. Write *v*, *n* or *adj* in the brackets after each gap.**

Health

1. Many people argue that standards in medical care are, in fact, in _____ (___) despite the many advances in medical treatment.

2. If the solution comes into _____ (___) with the eyes, rinse immediately with cold water.

3. The machine _____ (___) the patient's condition 24 hours a day.

4. Our _____ (___) concern is to ensure that all patients receive the best available treatment.

5. The surgery is open until late on _____ (___) days.

6. The number of people injured in the _____ (___) is continuing to rise and hospitals are finding it difficult to deal with the situation.

Business and Finance

7. John's application for a student loan has been _____ (___).

8. 'Link' is a cash machine _____ (___) connecting more than 41,000 ATMs.

9. Finding a suitable candidate for the position has proved a _____ (___).

10. Interest based on the amount of money originally invested and the interest already earned is known as _____ (___) interest.

11. It's very difficult to be _____ (___) when your own financial interests are involved.

12. The new saving account scheme is designed to _____ (___) a young audience.

3.3 Complete the sentences in Ex 3.2 with words from Ex 3.1. In the case of verbs, pay attention to the ending required, e.g., ~*s*, ~*ed*, ~*ing*. In the case of nouns, you may have to decide whether the singular or plural form is appropriate.

Task 4	Word families

Look at the following extract.

Whether the world is more prone to conflict than it used to be is hard to say. Perhaps we are just more <u>aware</u> of violent confrontation in different parts of the world. A famine in remote Sudan gets media coverage whereas a century ago starving populations might die unseen. Today's wars can be watched live on television, like Hollywood action movies. Greater <u>awareness</u> of the human consequences of battle may reduce the lust for war – or make it another spectator sport.

Source: Understanding Global Issues. (1998). *The Global Village: Challenges for a Shrinking Planet* [Pamphlet]. Buckley, R.

The underlined words are members of the same word family. As we have seen in previous units, this use of members of the same word family helps the author make the writing more cohesive.

4.1 Complete the table with these words. There may be some columns where there are two entries. You may know some other words to complete the light green cells.

modify	symbolic	logic	precisely	consultation	expansion
evolution	rejection	adjust	sustain	substitution	

Nouns	Verbs	Adjectives	Adverbs
modification			
symbol			
		sustainable	
	substitute		
		stable	

Nouns	Verbs	Adjectives	Adverbs
	reject		
precision			
	evolve		
			logically
	consult		
	expand		
adjustment			

4.2   **Choose the correct form of the word in brackets to complete the following sentences. In the case of verbs, pay attention to the ending required, e.g., ~s, ~ed, ~ing. In the case of nouns, you may have to decide whether the singular or plural form is appropriate.**

Economics

1.   There are no current plans to _____ monetary strategy. (alter)

2.   Many regions of the country are experiencing rapid economic _____. (expand)

3.   Once the _____ for inflation is taken into account, the fall in interest rates is quite small. (adjust)

4.   The importance of the city as a regional financial centre has _____ slowly. (evolve)

5.   _____ is paramount when calculating a budget. (precise)

6.   _____, companies need to invest money in marketing in order to grow. (logic)

Politics

7.   The long-term _____ of the currency remains the government's prime objective. (stable)

8.   Any attempt to reduce taxes would be seen as a _____ gesture from a government which is rapidly losing support. (symbol)

9.   Governments engaged in crop _____ programmes were promised extra assistance. (substitute)

10. The government's plans are a _____ of the policies of the previous regime. (reject)

11. The government is providing funding to _____ sporting facilities throughout the city. (sustain)

12. Their proposals will require some _____ before they can become law. (modify)

4.3 **Choose the correct form of the word in brackets to complete the sentences. In the case of verbs, pay attention to the ending required, e.g., ~ed, ~ing, ~s. In the case of nouns, you may have to decide whether the singular or plural form is appropriate.**

Business and Finance

1. Cranleigh Freight Services is planning to _____ into Eastern Europe, but some members of the management team have argued that such an _____ may not be in the best interests of the company. (expand)

2. It is often difficult to _____ to a change of career. Some people fail to make the _____ and simply go back to their old job. (adjust)

3. _____ in the exchange rate is a requirement for continued growth. A _____ currency will encourage investment. (stable)

4. In the modern world, businesses need to _____ rapidly, and without such an _____ they are unlikely to maintain their market share. (evolve)

Politics

5. Many people are still not _____ of the dangers of landmines, despite numerous government initiatives to raise _____. (aware)

6. The new plan has been drawn up in _____ with our Far Eastern partners. We attempted to _____ them at all stages of the project. (consult)

7. Living standards in Palestine are _____ rapidly. The main reason for this _____ is the continuing armed conflict in the region. (decline)

8. The US government claims that the weapons their planes use are very _____. The number of civilian casualties on the ground would suggest that this _____ is more theoretical than real. (precise)

Prefixes	
The following prefixes are used with a number of the words from AWL Sublist 5.	
Prefix	**Meaning**
re~	again
in~, un~, il~, im~	not, the opposite of

4.4   **Which of the prefixes above can be used with the following words?**

1. adjustment   _____

2. aware   _____

3. draft   _____

4. logical   _____

5. sustainable   _____

6. monitored   _____

7. precise   _____

8. stability   _____

4.5   **Complete the following sentences using either:**
- the correct form of the word in brackets; or
- a prefix + the correct form of the word in brackets

In the case of verbs, pay attention to the ending required, e.g., ~s, ~ed, ~ing.

Transport

1. Having a fear of flying is totally _____ given that statistics prove it is the safest form of transport. (logical)

2. We need transport policies that are both environmentally _____ and economically viable. (aware)

3. Parliament rejected the new transport bill, so the minister was forced to _____ it. (draft)

4. New technology means that the movements of aircraft can be _____ more closely than ever before. (monitor)

5. It may be environmentally friendly, but in the modern age, moving goods via the canal network is a totally _____ form of transport. (sustainable)

6. Financial _____ in the region is essential for investment in a modern transport system. (stability)

7. The receptionist's directions were both complicated and _____, with the result that I was late for the meeting. (precise)

Task 5	Collocations

Verbs and nouns

Look at these verb + noun combinations that appear in this unit.
- *make the transition*
- *reduce the number*

5.1   **Match the verbs on the left with the nouns on the right to make combinations from this unit.**

Verb		Noun
1. enforce	☐	a. welfare
2. reduce	☐	b. signs
3. show	☐	c. the transition
4. make	☐	d. taxes
5. face	☐	e. a challenge
6. threaten	☐	f. laws
7. safeguard	☐	g. awareness
8. facilitate	☐	h. input
9. exceed	☐	i. stability
10. raise	☐	j. work flow

5.2 **Choose the verb from the box that fits best with all the nouns in each group.**

alter	challenge	draft	generate
monitor	pursue	reject	sustain

1. _____ legislation, an agreement, a constitution, a letter

2. _____ an assumption, authority, a decision, leadership

3. _____ economic growth, life, interest, a level

4. _____ activity, progress, a situation

5. _____ revenue, jobs, new ideas, electricity

6. _____ an offer, an argument, a suggestion, a proposal, a request

7. _____ a career, a policy, a matter, an issue, interests

8. _____ a fact, a situation, behaviour, the way

5.3 **Complete the sentences below with an appropriate verb + noun combination from Ex 5.2. The first letter of each noun is given to help you. Pay attention to the form and tense of the verb in each sentence.**

1. They have set up a commission to _____
   a new c_____.

2. The government has _____ a
   p_____ to prohibit smoking in all
   workplaces, including bars and restaurants.

3. Service industries have _____
   thousands of new j_____ in recent years.

4. After the operation, the medical team has to
   _____ the patient's
   p_____ extremely carefully.

5. Local residents are unhappy that the court has
   decided to allow the new road to be built and have said that they plan to
   _____ the d_____ in a higher court.

6. As well as doing their school work, students are encouraged to _____
   their own i_____.

7. Increased consumer spending will help _____ the predicted e_____
   growth.

8. Nothing can _____ the f_____ that we are to blame.

Adjectives and nouns

Look at these adjective + noun combinations that appear in this unit.
- *new democracies*
- *personal perspective*

5.4 **Match the adjectives on the left with the nouns on the right to make combinations from this unit.**

Adjective		Noun
1. fundamental	☐	a. trends
2. present	☐	b. awareness
3. lost	☐	c. cause
4. different	☐	d. revenue
5. managerial	☐	e. staff
6. prime	☐	f. expansion
7. principal	☐	g. tasks
8. greater	☐	h. symbol
9. rapid economic	☐	i. versions

5.5 **Use your dictionary to find nouns that can be used with these adjectives.**

1. academic _____

2. stable _____

3. external _____

4. fundamental _____

5. prime _____

6. logical _____

7. objective _____

8. precise _____

5.6 **Look at the underlined words in the following sentences. Identify different combinations of verbs, nouns, adjectives, adverbs and prepositions. Then answer the questions that follow.**

Politics

1. The conflict is rapidly <u>evolving</u> into a civil war.

2. The United Nations is <u>monitoring</u> the situation very closely.

3. Local journalists argue that the conflict has to be seen from a historical <u>perspective</u>.

4. The country has found it extremely difficult to make the <u>transition</u> from a dependent colony to a democracy.

5. Meanwhile, the government is trying to improve its <u>image</u> overseas.

6. According to the official <u>version</u> of events, the recent clashes in the west of the country were caused by 'criminal gangs'.

Business and Finance

7. The local economy <u>expanded</u> rapidly during the 1980s and 1990s, but is currently in a period of crisis.

8. Businessmen and entrepreneurs have frequently come into <u>conflict</u> with politicians as new laws are introduced.

9. Many factories in the country are now working at a reduced <u>capacity</u>.

10. The company has the <u>capacity</u> to build 3,000 cars a month.

11. The same process has been used for almost 20 years with only minor <u>modifications</u>.

12. The company has made a number of <u>modifications</u> to their latest model to maximize passenger safety.

13. The company has also made a slight <u>adjustment</u> to the engine.

14. Strong sales in the domestic sector have led to plans to <u>expand</u> overseas.

15. The company hopes to reach its <u>target</u> of 15 per cent growth this year.

16. Car buyers are becoming increasingly environmentally <u>aware</u>.

17. Green issues have given many consumers a new <u>perspective</u> on their everyday transport needs.

Questions:

a. What verbs are used with these nouns (either before or after)?

an adjustment   _____

transition   _____

capacity   _____

image   _____

conflict (with)   _____

modifications   _____

its target   _____

b. What adjectives are used with these nouns?

adjustment   _____

(at) ~ capacity   _____

perspective   _____

version   _____

modifications   _____

c. What adverbs are used with these words (either before or after)?

evolving   _____

aware   _____

expanded   _____

monitoring   _____

> **Study tip**
>
> With the verbs _evolving_ and _monitoring,_ the adverb could also appear in the other position, i.e., _evolve gradually, closely monitor._

Task 6   Word grammar

Discovering noun patterns

You studied the following patterns in Unit 5. Ex 6.1 will help you notice these patterns in the texts you read.

- noun + preposition, e.g., _decline in_
- noun followed by _that_, e.g., _the notion that_
- noun followed by _to_ + infinitive, e.g., _capacity to invest_
- noun followed by _to be_ + _that_ + clause, e.g., _trend is that …_

6.1 **Look at the underlined nouns in the sentences below and answer the following questions.**

1. Is a preposition used to connect the underlined noun to the following noun or gerund (e.g., *hiring*)? If so, what preposition?

a. _____   b. _____   c. _____   d. _____   e. _____   f. _____

g. _____   h. _____   i. _____   j. _____   k. _____   l. _____

m. _____   n. _____   o. _____   p. _____   q. _____   r. _____

s. _____   t. _____

2. Which noun is followed by *that* + clause?

_____

3. Which noun is followed by the verb *to be* + *that* + clause?

_____

4. What prepositions come before *consultation* and *target*?

_____

5. Which noun is followed by *to* + infinitive?

_____

Current Affairs

a. The government is concerned about its <u>capacity</u> to invest in the country's infrastructure.

b. A lot of money has been invested in promoting a more positive <u>image</u> of the country.

c. The <u>notion</u> that the country can recover from its economic problems within the next two years is quite absurd.

d. The system in many countries is far removed from classical <u>notions</u> of democracy.

e. The rapid <u>expansion</u> of Mexico City led to social and economic problems.

f. The government will fail to meet its <u>target</u> of reducing greenhouse gas emissions by ten per cent this year.

Business

g. The <u>transition</u> from a state-owned business to a private company can be extremely difficult.

h. The plans were drawn up in <u>consultation</u> with our overseas partners.

i. The company is now ready to meet the <u>challenges</u> of a highly competitive market.

j. There has been a significant <u>expansion</u> in the number of software companies operating in this field.

k. Many companies operate on a gross profit <u>margin</u> of less than five per cent.

l. Sales last year were five per cent below <u>target</u>.

m. The company says it is on <u>target</u> for a 20 per cent increase in sales this year.

Health

n. Prolonged <u>exposure</u> to other people's cigarette smoke can cause serious health problems.

o. Most people have an <u>awareness</u> of the dangers of passive smoking.

p. Millions of dollars have been invested in schemes to raise <u>awareness</u> about AIDS in Africa.

q. The hospital has a <u>capacity</u> of 500 beds.

r. There has been a dramatic <u>decline</u> in the number of jobs in the public health sector.

s. In recent years, there has been an increasing <u>trend</u> of women in the UK giving birth at home.

t. One worrying <u>trend</u> is that children are not doing enough exercise outside school.

6.2 **Look back at the previous exercises in this unit and check which prepositions are used to connect these nouns with following nouns or gerunds.**

1. ratio   *of*_____

2. welfare   _____

3. symbol   _____

4. generation   _____

5. version   _____

6. adjustment   _____

7. perspective   _____

Noun + noun combinations

Here are some examples of noun + noun combinations from previous exercises in this unit.
- *budget air travel*
- *market economy*
- *fossil fuels*
- *airline passengers*

6.3   **Match the nouns on the left with the nouns on the right to make noun + noun combinations from this unit.**

Noun 1		Noun 2
1. air	☐	a. fuel
2. work	☐	b. needs
3. aviation	☐	c. target
4. exchange	☐	d. flow
5. transport	☐	e. safety
6. passenger	☐	f. travel
7. freedom	☐	g. rate
8. Internet	☐	h. access
9. sales	☐	i. rates
10. interest	☐	j. fighter

Note: For more information about noun patterns, see Unit 5.

6.4   **Use your dictionary to find nouns that can be used in combination with the following nouns (either before or after).**

1. target _____

2. substitute _____

3. energy _____

4. network _____

5. margin _____

Discovering adjective patterns

We saw in Unit 9, Ex 6.4, how some adjectives can be followed by (*that*) + clause or by a verb phrase. In this exercise, we will look at other adjectives and how they are used in sentences.

6.5 **Look at the underlined words in the sentences below and answer the following questions.**

Health

1. Twenty minutes' exercise on this machine is <u>equivalent</u> to walking five kilometres.

2. Most people are well <u>aware</u> that regular exercise promotes good health.

3. Many people are <u>aware</u> of the benefits of a healthy diet combined with exercise.

4. Running or jogging for at least 20 minutes three times a week is <u>fundamental</u> to building up a good physical condition.

5. It is <u>logical</u> to start with gentle exercise and then build up the routine over a number of weeks.

6. It is difficult to be <u>precise</u> about the number of calories different sporting activities can burn off.

7. It may seem <u>logical</u> that if output exceeds input you will lose weight but, unfortunately, this does not always happen.

8. The current obsession with dieting is <u>symbolic</u> of an age when image is everything.

Questions:

a. Which adjectives are followed by *to* + infinitive?

_____

b. Which adjectives are followed by *that* + clause?

_____

c. Which prepositions are used to connect the adjectives to noun phrases?

_____

Transitive or intransitive verbs

In earlier exercises in this unit, we have seen examples of the following verbs which show that they can be used with noun phrases as objects: *enforce, facilitate, modify, reject, target, monitor, alter, sustain, draft, challenge, generate, pursue.*

Examples:
- *enforce laws*
- *facilitate work flow*
- *parking regulations will be strictly enforced*
- *modify their travel habits*

Notice that in the third example the verb *enforced* is used passively. All transitive verbs can be used passively.

6.6   **Here are some other verbs from AWL Sublist 5 which are either always transitive or always intransitive. Complete the tables below by putting the verbs in the correct column.**

amend	conflict	contact	compound
expose	liberalize	enable	license	symbolize

Transitive verbs	Intransitive verbs

6.7   **Copy an example sentence from your dictionary for each of the transitive verbs from the completed table in Ex 6.6.**

_____

_____

_____

_____

_____

_____

_____

_____

_____

_____

_____

_____

_____

6.8   **Copy an example sentence from your dictionary for each of the intransitive verbs from the completed table in Ex 6.6.**

_____

_____

_____

_____

_____

_____

_____

_____

_____

_____

_____

_____

Verbs that are both transitive and intransitive
The following verbs are sometimes transitive and sometimes intransitive: _adjust, alter, consult, decline, expand, evolve, stabilize, substitute._

6.9   **Look at the verbs as they are used in these sentences and decide if they are transitive (VT) or intransitive (VI).**

Social Science

1.   An increasing number of people are choosing to <u>alter</u> their appearance with cosmetic surgery. (___)

2.   The number of people owning their own homes has <u>declined</u> by ten per cent. (___)

3.   The president <u>declined</u> an invitation to the conference. (___)

4.   The manufacturers have stopped using steel and <u>substituted</u> a lighter and more flexible material. (___)

5.   Teachers must <u>evolve</u> new ways of teaching Information Technology, as computers become more advanced every day. (___)

6. Software will continue to <u>evolve</u> as consumers demand more effective solutions. (___)

7. When gold was discovered in the area, California <u>expanded</u> rapidly and soon started to prosper. (___)

Economics

8. The government is planning to <u>expand</u> trade by opening up new markets. (___)

9. The researchers <u>consulted</u> with a number of representatives from different sectors of the economy. (___)

10. This Economics book is not a reliable source, as no experts were <u>consulted</u> when it was written. (___)

11. New regulations are needed to help <u>stabilize</u> the economy. (___)

12. Interest rates have now <u>stabilized</u>. (___)

13. Businesses need time to <u>adjust</u> to changing economic circumstances. (___)

14. The latest figures have been <u>adjusted</u> to take account of inflation. (___)

Task 7	Review

It is important you find time to review the exercises you have done in this unit and review what you have learnt.

7.1   Look back through the unit and find:

1. five adjective + noun collocations

_____

_____

2. five noun + noun collocations

_____

_____

3. five nouns often followed by prepositions

_____

_____

4. five words that can be either nouns or verbs

_____

_____

7.2 **Look back over all the exercises you have done and write down phrases that you think are useful and that you want to remember.**

Examples:

… reject suggestions that …

… nothing can alter the fact that …

… sustain economic growth …

… make a slight adjustment to …

… make the transition from … to …

Make your own notes here.

_____

_____

_____

_____

_____

_____

_____

_____

_____

_____

_____

_____

_____

_____

7.3 **Look at AWL Sublist 5 on pages 176–177. Check the words you don't know in your dictionary and make notes on the meanings and use of the words.**

Example:

Word (word class)	Meaning
entity	something that exists as a separate and complete unit

Example sentences:

The province has now become a separate entity.

The four sections have been brought together as a single entity.

Make your own notes here.

_____

_____

_____

_____

_____

_____

_____

_____

_____

_____

_____

_____

_____

_____

_____

_____

_____

_____

_____

_____

Vocabulary List

Business and Finance
advertising
bank lending rate
currency
domestic sector
entrepreneur
financial centre
gross profit margin
interest rate
market economy
monetary strategy
revenue
state-owned business
strike (n)
tax revenue
work flow

Environment
carbon emission
environmentally aware
environmentally
  friendly
green issue
wind farm

Health
welfare

Politics
bill
colony
commission
communist regime
constitution
democracy
freedom fighter
government initiative
Marxist
nationalism
terrorist
United Nations

Science
air pressure
atom
element
evolution

Society
citizen
living standards
local resident

Verbs
argue
claim
coexist
earn
engage (in)
fail
preserve
pursue
safeguard
supply
switch
threaten

Other
absurd
activist
armed conflict
aviation fuel

bulky
civil war
civilian casualties
competitive
considerable
dependent
description
input (n)
interconnected
Internet access
journalist
landmine
long-haul flight
modern era
open-minded
outstanding natural
  beauty
prime objective
prone to
stringently
survival
viable

For web resources relevant to this book, see:
www.englishforacademicstudy.com

These weblinks will give you access to gap-fill exercises to review and recycle the general word families contained within the AWL; numerous vocabulary lists, explanations, games and crosswords; and a comprehensive section on the AWL.

Glossary

Academic Word List (AWL)

A list of some of the most wide-ranging and frequently used English words in academic contexts. Students can use the AWL to find the most useful academic words that they need to know when they study at an English-speaking university.

achievement test

An assessment form that tests what someone has learnt and shows them what they have achieved on a course or during a specific period of time.

antonym

A word that has the opposite meaning to another. For example, *big* is an antonym of *small*.

clause

A group of words including a subject and a finite verb that form part of a sentence. A main clause can form a sentence on its own, but a dependent clause needs to have a main clause with it to form a sentence.

cohesion

Cohesion is the way that words and ideas are linked together in a text. It includes repetition of words and the use of synonyms, referencing words such as pronouns and the use of different word classes.

collocation

The way that certain words are habitually used together, e.g., *strong cheese* and *fish and chips* collocate, but not *weak cheese* or *chips and fish*.

complement

A word or phrase that follows the verb to complete a sentence. The complement describes the subject of the sentence, e.g., *John is highly qualified* (the complement is an adjective); *John became a doctor* (the complement is a noun).

corpus

A large collection of language (written texts or spoken recordings) that can be used for linguistic analysis.

(dictionary) entry

The section of a dictionary that gives a definition and information about a word.

General Service List (GSL)

A list of over 2,000 word families that are used frequently in a wide variety of general and academic texts.

gerund

A word ending in *~ing* that acts as a noun but is formed from a verb, e.g., *Studying abroad can be difficult.*

headword

In a dictionary, the headword is usually in large or bold type so that it is easy to locate.

homonym

Two (or more) words that are spelt and pronounced the same way but have different, unrelated meanings, e.g., *bank: He sat on the bank of the river. I borrowed some money from the bank.*

intransitive verb

A verb that either cannot or does not need to take an object, e.g., *rain, agree: It rained. She agreed.*

monolingual dictionary

A dictionary that only uses the same language for the word and its definition, e.g., English-English, not a translation into another language.

multi-meaning words

Words that have two or more meanings. These may be polysemes with related meanings, e.g., *primary* has several meanings, all related to beginnings; they can also be homonyms with unrelated meanings.

non-detachable word parts

Word parts that cannot be separated from a word and form another complete word, e.g., *dis~*.

noun phrase

A phrase in which a noun (or pronoun) is the headword, e.g., *a substance: this substance, a chemical substance.*

passive

The passive (passive voice) is a way of constructing a sentence so that the emphasis is not on the agent of an action or process, but on the thing or person that has been affected or acted upon, e.g., compare: *An experiment was conducted* (passive). *We conducted an experiment* (active).

phrase

A group of words that function together as a unit. A phrase does not contain both a subject and a verb form, so cannot form a full clause or sentence.

polyseme

A word or phrase that has several meanings that may be related to each other. In a dictionary, a polysemous word will have all its different forms and meanings listed under the same headword.

prefix

A letter or group of letters that can be added to the start of a word to change its meaning, e.g., *un~*, *im~*, *dis~*, *re~*.

root (of a word)

The source or origin of a word. Other words develop from the root using prefixes and suffixes, e.g., words such as *review*, *preview*, *viewer* developed from the root word *view*.

stress

Word stress is the way that one syllable is given more force in a word. Stressed syllables or words are louder and longer than unstressed syllables. English places stresses on key words or new information in a sentence, so it is important to learn to recognize stressed words.

suffix

A letter or group of letters that can be added to the end of the word to change its meaning, word class or grammatical function, e.g., *~less*, *~ful*, *~ed*.

syllable

A unit of sound in a word. Each syllable has a vowel at its centre and consonants 'surround' the vowel. It is also possible to have a syllable with just a vowel. For example, the word *any* has two syllables (*a-ny*).

synonym

A word that has the same or a similar meaning to another word. For example, *amiable* is a synonym of *friendly*.

terminology

Vocabulary (or terms) used in a particular field, topic or area of study. These may be technical words or terms to describe complex concepts that are specific to that topic.

transitive verb

A verb that needs to take an object, e.g., it is not possible to use the verb *send* in a sentence without an object: *He sent his report* (object).

word class

Word classes are used to categorize words in terms of which parts of speech they are, i.e., whether they are nouns, adjectives, verbs, etc. For example, the word class of *window* is noun.

word family

A group of words that are closely related to each other because they share a common root or because they have related meanings, e.g., *family, familiar, familiarize, familiarization*.

word grammar

The way that individual words are used in sentences and how they connect with other words, or with other parts of the sentence, e.g., the verb patterns associated with the word, the way it changes when used in other word classes.

On the following pages you will find all the members of the word families in the first five sublists of the Academic Word List.

Each word in italics is the most frequently occurring member of the word family in the Academic Corpus. For example, *analysis* is the most common form of the word family 'analyze'. British and American spellings are included in the word families, so 'contextualise' and 'contextualize' are both included in the family *context*.

Appendix 1: Academic Word List

Sublist 1 (Unit 6)

analyze
analysed
analyser
analysers
analyses
analysing
analysis
analyst
analysts
analytic
analytical
analytically
analyze
analyzed
analyzes
analyzing

approach
approachable
approached
approaches
approaching
unapproachable

area
areas

assess
assessable
assessed
assesses
assessing
assessment
assessments
reassess
reassessed
reassessing
reassessment
unassessed

assume
assumed

assumes
assuming
assumption
assumptions

authority
authoritative
authorities

available
availability
unavailable

benefit
beneficial
beneficiary
beneficiaries
benefited
benefiting
benefits

concept
conception
concepts
conceptual
conceptualisation
conceptualise
conceptualised
conceptualises
conceptualising
conceptualization
conceptualize
conceptualized
conceptualizes
conceptualizing
conceptually

consist
consisted
consistency
consistent
consistently
consisting
consists

inconsistencies
inconsistency
inconsistent

constitute
constituencies
constituency
constituent
constituents
constituted
constitutes
constituting
constitution
constitutions
constitutional
constitutionally
constitutive
unconstitutional

context
contexts
contextual
contextualise
contextualised
contextualising
uncontextualised
contextualize
contextualized
contextualizing
uncontextualized

contract
contracted
contracting
contractor
contractors
contracts

create
created
creates
creating
creation
creations

creative
creatively
creativity
creator
creators
recreate
recreated
recreates
recreating

data

define
definable
defined
defines
defining
definition
definitions
redefine
redefined
redefines
redefining
undefined

derive
derivation
derivations
derivative
derivatives
derived
derives
deriving

distribute
distributed
distributing
distribution
distributional
distributions
distributive
distributor
distributors
redistribute

redistributed
redistributes
redistributing
redistribution

economy
economic
economical
economically
economics
economies
economist
economists
uneconomical

environment
environmental
environmentalist
environmentalists
environmentally
environments

establish
disestablish
disestablished
disestablishes
disestablishing
disestablishment
established
establishes
establishing
establishment
establishments

estimate
estimated
estimates
estimating
estimation
estimations
overestimate
overestimated
overestimates
overestimating
underestimate
underestimated
underestimates
underestimating

evident
evidenced
evidence
evidential
evidently

export
exported
exporter
exporters

exporting
exports

factor
factored
factoring
factors

finance
financed
finances
financial
financially
financier
financiers
financing

formula
formulae
formulas
formulate
formulated
formulating
formulation
formulations
reformulate
reformulated
reformulating
reformulation
reformulations

function
functional
functionally
functionality
functioned
functioning
functions

identify
identifiable
identification
identified
identifies
identifying
identities
identity
unidentifiable

income
incomes

indicate
indicated
indicates
indicating
indication
indications
indicative
indicator

indicators
individual
individualisation
individualise
individualised
individualises
individualising
individualism
individualist
individualistic
individualists
individuality
individualization
individualize
individualized
individualizes
individualizing
individually
individuals

interpret
interpretation
interpretations
interpretative
interpreted
interpreting
interpretive
interprets
misinterpret
misinterpretation
misinterpretations
misinterpreted
misinterpreting
misinterprets
reinterpret
reinterpreted
reinterprets
reinterpreting
reinterpretation
reinterpretations

involve
involved
involvement
involves
involving
uninvolved

issue
issued
issues
issuing

labour
labor
labored
laboring

labors
laboured
labouring
labours

legal
illegal
illegality
illegally
legality
legally

legislate
legislated
legislates
legislating
legislation
legislative
legislator
legislators
legislature

major
majorities
majority

method
methodical
methodological
methodologies
methodology
methods

occur
occurred
occurrence
occurrences
occurring
occurs
reoccur
reoccurred
reoccurring
reoccurs

per cent
percentage
percentages

period
periodic
periodical
periodically
periodicals
periods

policy
policies

principle
principled
principles
unprincipled

proceed
procedural
procedure
procedures
proceeded
proceeding
proceedings
proceeds

process
processed
processes
processing

require
required
requirement
requirements
requires
requiring

research
researched
researcher
researchers
researches
researching

respond
responded
respondent
respondents
responding
responds
response
responses
responsive
responsiveness
unresponsive

role
roles

section
sectioned
sectioning
sections

sector
sectors

significant
insignificant
insignificantly
significance
significantly
signified
signifies
signify
signifying

similar
dissimilar
similarities
similarity
similarly

source
sourced
sources
sourcing

specific
specifically
specification
specifications
specificity
specifics

structure
restructure
restructured
restructures
restructuring
structural
structurally
structured
structures
structuring
unstructured

theory
theoretical
theoretically
theories
theorist
theorists

vary
invariable
invariably
variability
variable
variables
variably
variance
variant
variants
variation
variations
varied
varies
varying

Sublist 2 (Unit 7)

achieve
achievable
achieved
achievement
achievements
achieves
achieving

acquire
acquired
acquires
acquiring
acquisition
acquisitions

administrate
administrates
administration
administrations
administrative
administratively
administrator
administrators

affect
affected
affecting
affective
affectively
affects
unaffected

appropriate
appropriacy
appropriately
appropriateness
inappropriacy
inappropriate
inappropriately

aspect
aspects

assist
assistance
assistant
assistants
assisted
assisting
assists
unassisted

category
categories
categorisation
categorise
categorised
categorises
categorising

categorization
categorize
categorized
categorizes
categorizing

chapter
chapters

commission
commissioned
commissioner
commissioners
commissioning
commissions

community
communities

complex
complexities
complexity

compute
computation
computational
computations
computable
computer
computed
computerised
computerized
computers
computing

conclude
concluded
concludes
concluding
conclusion
conclusions
conclusive
conclusively
inconclusive
inconclusively

conduct
conducted
conducting
conducts

consequent
consequence
consequences
consequently

construct
constructed
constructing
construction
constructions
constructive

constructs
reconstruct
reconstructed
reconstructing
reconstruction
reconstructs

consume
consumed
consumer
consumers
consumes
consuming
consumption

credit
credited
crediting
creditor
creditors
credits

culture
cultural
culturally
cultured
cultures
uncultured

design
designed
designer
designers
designing
designs

distinct
distinction
distinctions
distinctive
distinctively
distinctly
indistinct
indistinctly

element
elements

equate
equated
equates
equating
equation
equations

evaluate
evaluated
evaluates
evaluating
evaluation
evaluations

evaluative
re-evaluate
re-evaluated
re-evaluates
re-evaluating
re-evaluation

feature
featured
features
featuring

final
finalise
finalised
finalises
finalising
finalize
finalized
finalizes
finalizing
finality
finally
finals

focus
focused
focuses
focusing
focussed
focusses
focussing
refocus
refocused
refocuses
refocusing
refocussed
refocusses
refocussing

impact
impacted
impacting
impacts

injure
injured
injures
injuries
injuring
injury
uninjured

institute
instituted
institutes
instituting
institution
institutional
institutionalise

institutionalised
institutionalises
institutionalising
institutionalize
institutionalized
institutionalizes
institutionalizing
institutionally
institutions

invest
invested
investing
investment
investments
investor
investors
invests
reinvest
reinvested
reinvesting
reinvestment
reinvests

item
itemisation
itemise
itemised
itemises
itemising
itemization
itemize
itemized
itemizes
itemizing
items

journal
journals

maintain
maintained
maintaining
maintains
maintenance

normal
abnormal
abnormally
normalisation
normalise
normalised
normalises
normalising
normalization

normalize
normalized
normalizes
normalizing
normality
normally

obtain
obtainable
obtained
obtaining
obtains
unobtainable

participate
participant
participants
participated
participates
participating
participation
participatory

perceive
perceived
perceives
perceiving
perception
perceptions

positive
positively

potential
potentially

previous
previously

primary
primarily

purchase
purchased
purchaser
purchasers
purchases
purchasing

range
ranged
ranges
ranging

region
regional
regionally
regions

regulate
deregulated
deregulates
deregulating
deregulation
regulated
regulates
regulating
regulation
regulations
regulator
regulators
regulatory
unregulated

relevant
irrelevance
irrelevant
relevance

reside
resided
residence
resident
residential
residents
resides
residing

resource
resourced
resourceful
resources
resourcing
unresourceful
under-resourced

restrict
restricted
restricting
restriction
restrictions
restrictive
restrictively
restricts
unrestricted
unrestrictive

secure
insecure
insecurities
insecurity
secured
securely
secures

securing
securities
security

seek
seeking
seeks
sought

select
selected
selecting
selection
selections
selective
selectively
selector
selectors
selects

site
sites

strategy
strategic
strategies
strategically
strategist
strategists

survey
surveyed
surveying
surveys

text
texts
textual

tradition
non-traditional
traditional
traditionalist
traditionally
traditions

transfer
transferable
transference
transferred
transferring
transfers

Sublist 3 (Unit 8)

alternative
alternatively
alternatives

circumstance
circumstances

comment
commentaries
commentary
commentator
commentators
commented
commenting
comments

compensate
compensated
compensates
compensating
compensation
compensations
compensatory

component
componentry
components

consent
consensus
consented
consenting
consents

considerable
considerably

constant
constancy
constantly
constants
inconstancy
inconstantly

constrain
constrained
constraining
constrains
constraint
constraints
unconstrained

contribute
contributed
contributes
contributing
contribution
contributions
contributor
contributors

convene
convention
convenes
convened
convening
conventional
conventionally
conventions
unconventional

coordinate
coordinated
coordinates
coordinating
coordination
coordinator
coordinators
co-ordinate
co-ordinated
co-ordinates
co-ordinating
co-ordination
co-ordinator
co-ordinators

core
cores
coring
cored

corporate
corporates
corporation
corporations

correspond
corresponded
correspondence
corresponding
correspondingly
corresponds

criteria
criterion

deduce
deduced
deduces
deducing
deduction
deductions

demonstrate
demonstrable
demonstrably
demonstrated
demonstrates
demonstrating
demonstration
demonstrations

demonstrative
demonstratively
demonstrator
demonstrators

document
documentation
documented
documenting
documents

dominate
dominance
dominant
dominated
dominates
dominating
domination

emphasis
emphasise
emphasised
emphasising
emphasize
emphasized
emphasizes
emphasizing
emphatic
emphatically

ensure
ensured
ensures
ensuring

exclude
excluded
excludes
excluding
exclusion
exclusionary
exclusionist
exclusions
exclusive
exclusively

framework
frameworks

fund
funded
funder
funders
funding
funds

illustrate
illustrated
illustrates
illustrating
illustration

illustrations
illustrative

immigrate
immigrant
immigrants
immigrated
immigrates
immigrating
immigration

imply
implied
implies
implying

initial
initially

instance
instances

interact
interacted
interacting
interaction
interactions
interactive
interactively
interacts

justify
justifiable
justifiably
justification
justifications
justified
justifies
justifying
unjustified

layer
layered
layering
layers

link
linkage
linkages
linked
linking
links

locate
located
locating
location
locations
relocate
relocated
relocates

relocating
relocation

maximise
max
maximised
maximises
maximising
maximisation
maximize
maximized
maximizes
maximizing
maximization
maximum

minor
minorities
minority
minors

negate
negative
negated
negates
negating
negatively
negatives

outcome
outcomes

partner
partners
partnership
partnerships

philosophy
philosopher
philosophers
philosophical
philosophically
philosophies
philosophise
philosophised
philosophises

philosophising
philosophize
philosophized
philosophizes
philosophizing

physical
physically

proportion
disproportion
disproportionate
disproportionately
proportional
proportionally
proportionate
proportionately
proportions

publish
published
publisher
publishers
publishes
publishing
unpublished

react
reacted
reacts
reacting
reaction
reactionaries
reactionary
reactions
reactive
reactivate
reactivation
reactor
reactors

register
deregister
deregistered
deregistering
deregisters

deregistration
registered
registering
registers
registration

rely
reliability
reliable
reliably
reliance
reliant
relied
relies
relying
unreliable

remove
removable
removal
removals
removed
removes
removing

scheme
schematic
schematically
schemed
schemes
scheming

sequence
sequenced
sequences
sequencing
sequential
sequentially

sex
sexes
sexism
sexual
sexuality
sexually

shift
shifted
shifting
shifts

specify
specifiable
specified
specifies
specifying
unspecified

sufficient
sufficiency
insufficient
insufficiently
sufficiently

task
tasks

technical
technically

technique
techniques

technology
technological
technologically

valid
invalidate
invalidity
validate
validated
validating
validation
validity
validly

volume
volumes
vol.

Sublist 4 (Unit 9)

access
accessed
accesses
accessibility
accessible
accessing
inaccessible

adequate
adequacy
adequately
inadequacies
inadequacy
inadequate
inadequately

annual
annually

apparent
apparently

approximate
approximated
approximately
approximates
approximating
approximation
approximations

attitude
attitudes

attribute
attributable
attributed
attributes
attributing
attribution

civil

code
coded
codes
coding

commit
commitment
commitments
commits
committed
committing

communicate
communicable
communicated
communicates
communicating
communication
communications

communicative
communicatively
uncommunicative

concentrate
concentrated
concentrates
concentrating
concentration

confer
conference
conferences
conferred
conferring
confers

contrast
contrasted
contrasting
contrastive
contrasts

cycle
cycled
cycles
cyclic
cyclical
cycling

debate
debatable
debated
debates
debating

despite

dimension
dimensional
dimensions
multidimensional

domestic
domestically
domesticate
domesticated
domesticating
domestics

emerge
emerged
emergence
emergent
emerges
emerging

error
erroneous
erroneously
errors

ethnic
ethnicity

goal
goals

grant
granted
granting
grants

hence

hypothesis
hypotheses
hypothesise
hypothesised
hypothesises
hypothesising
hypothesize
hypothesized
hypothesizes
hypothesizing
hypothetical
hypothetically

implement
implementation
implemented
implementing
implements

implicate
implicated
implicates
implicating
implication
implications

impose
imposed
imposes
imposing
imposition

integrate
integrated
integrates
integrating
integration

internal
internalise
internalised
internalises
internalising
internalize
internalized
internalizes
internalizing
internally

investigate
investigated
investigates
investigating
investigation
investigations
investigative
investigator
investigators

job
jobs

label
labeled
labeling
labelled
labelling
labels

mechanism
mechanisms

obvious
obviously

occupy
occupancy
occupant
occupants
occupation
occupational
occupations
occupied
occupier
occupiers
occupies
occupying

option
optional
options

output
outputs

overall

parallel
paralleled
parallelled
paralleling
parallelling
parallels
unparalleled
unparaleled

parameter
parameters

phase
phased
phases
phasing

predict
predictability
predictable
predictably
predicted
predicting
prediction
predictions
predicts
unpredictability
unpredictable

principal
principally

prior

professional
professionally
professionals
professionalism

project
projected
projecting

projection
projections
projects

promote
promoted
promoter
promoters
promotes
promoting
promotion
promotions

regime
regimes

resolve
resolution
resolved
resolves
resolving
unresolved

retain
retained
retaining
retainer
retainers
retains

retention
retentive

series

statistic
statistician
statisticians
statistical
statistically
statistics

status

stress
stressed
stresses
stressful
stressing
unstressed

subsequent
subsequently

sum
summation
summed
summing
sums

summary
summaries
summarise
summarised
summarises
summarising
summarisation
summarisations
summarization
summarizations
summarize
summarized
summarizes
summarizing

undertake
undertaken
undertakes
undertaking
undertook

Sublist 5 (Unit 10)

academy
academia
academic
academically
academics
academies

adjust
adjusted
adjusting
adjustment
adjustments
adjusts
readjust
readjusted
readjusting
readjustment
readjustments
readjusts

alter
alterable
alteration
alterations
altered
altering
alternate
alternating
alters
unalterable
unaltered

amend
amended
amending
amendment
amendments
amends

aware
awareness
unaware

capacity
capacities
incapacitate
incapacitated

challenge
challenged
challenger
challengers
challenges
challenging

clause
clauses

compound
compounded
compounding
compounds

conflict
conflicted
conflicting
conflicts

consult
consultancy
consultant
consultants
consultation
consultations
consultative
consulted
consults
consulting

contact
contactable
contacted
contacting
contacts

decline
declined
declines
declining

discrete
discretely
discretion
discretionary
indiscrete
indiscretion

draft
drafted
drafting
drafts
redraft
redrafted
redrafting
redrafts

enable
enabled
enables
enabling

energy
energetic
energetically
energies

enforce
enforced
enforcement
enforces
enforcing

entity
entities

equivalent
equivalence

evolve
evolution
evolved
evolving
evolves
evolutionary
evolutionist
evolutionists

expand
expanded
expanding
expands
expansion
expansionism
expansive

expose
exposed
exposes
exposing
exposure
exposures

external
externalisation
externalise
externalised
externalises
externalising
externality
externalization
externalize
externalized
externalizes
externalizing
externally

facilitate
facilitated
facilitates
facilities
facilitating
facilitation
facilitator
facilitators
facility

fundamental
fundamentally

generate
generated
generates
generating

generation
generations

image
imagery
images

liberal
liberalise
liberalism
liberalisation
liberalised
liberalises
liberalising
liberalization
liberalize
liberalized
liberalizes
liberalizing
liberate
liberated
liberates
liberation
liberations
liberating
liberator
liberators
liberally
liberals

licence
licences
license
licensed
licensing
licenses
unlicensed

logic
illogical
illogically
logical
logically
logician
logicians

margin
marginal
marginally
margins

medical
medically

mental
mentality
mentally

modify
modification
modifications
modified
modifies
modifying
unmodified

monitor
monitored
monitoring
monitors
unmonitored

network
networked
networking
networks

notion
notions

objective
objectively
objectivity

orient
orientate
orientated
orientates
orientation
orientating
oriented
orienting
orients
reorient
reorientation

perspective
perspectives

precise
imprecise
precisely
precision

prime
primacy

psychology
psychological
psychologically
psychologist
psychologists

pursue
pursued
pursues
pursuing
pursuit
pursuits

ratio
ratios

reject
rejected
rejecting
rejection
rejects
rejections

revenue
revenues

stable
instability
stabilisation
stabilise
stabilised
stabilises
stabilising
stabilization
stabilize
stabilized

stabilizes
stabilizing
stability
unstable

style
styled
styles
styling
stylish
stylise
stylised
stylises
stylising
stylize
stylized
stylizes
stylizing

substitute
substituted
substitutes
substituting
substitution

sustain
sustainable
sustainability
sustained
sustaining
sustains
sustenance
unsustainable

symbol
symbolic
symbolically
symbolise
symbolises
symbolised
symbolising
symbolism

symbolize
symbolized
symbolizes
symbolizing
symbols

target
targeted
targeting
targets

transit
transited
transiting
transition
transitional
transitions
transitory
transits

trend
trends

version
versions

welfare

whereas

Appendix 2: Achievement test

In this test you will:
- check your knowledge of the words in the Academic Word List
- check the progress you have made in understanding these words

There is no time limit for this test. The point of the test is to allow you to assess how much you have learnt by studying this book, and to give you an idea of what you need to look at again.

All the words and sentences in this test are taken from Units 6–10.

We suggest you complete the test and then check the answers at the back of the book. If you make any mistakes, you can go back and look at Units 6–10.

Task 1	Meanings of words

1.1 **Complete the pairs of sentences below with a word from the box. In each pair, you need the same word for both sentences. In the case of verbs, pay attention to the ending required, e.g., ~s, ~ed, ~ing. In the case of nouns, you may have to decide whether the singular or plural form is appropriate.**

dominant	~~available~~	restrict	apparent	aware	vary

1. Information about this product is freely _____available_____ on the Internet.

   Updates are _____available_____ from our website.

2. Demand for particular products _____ with the seasons.

   Pay levels may _____ slightly, depending on relevant experience.

3. Many countries _____ smoking in public places such as bars and restaurants.

   Smoking is _____ to designated areas.

4. The company is trying to maintain its _____ position in the market.

   Ten years ago, the company enjoyed a _____ share of the market.

5. It was soon _____ that there was a serious problem with the onboard equipment.

   The flight was cancelled for no _____ reason.

6. Few people are _____ of the dangers a sudden change in air pressure can cause.

   Tim suddenly became _____ of someone following him.

Task 2   Multi-meaning words

2.1   **Choose the correct meaning of the underlined words according to the context in which they appear.**

1.   It doesn't matter which <u>order</u> you answer the questions in.
   - a.   the way that things or events are arranged in relation to each other, for example, showing whether something is first, second, third, etc.
   - b.   an instruction to do something that is given by someone in authority
   - c.   a request for food or drink in a restaurant or bar

2.   Perhaps the most obvious sign of globalization is in the economic <u>area</u>.
   - a.   a particular part of a city, town, region or country
   - b.   the amount of space covered by the surface of a place or shape
   - c.   a particular subject or range of activities

3.   Developed countries <u>consume</u> huge quantities of raw materials.
   - a.   to make use of a quantity of something
   - b.   to eat or drink something
   - c.   to permanently use something up

4.   A number of different human activities have <u>contributed</u> to climate change.
   - a.   to add your money, goods, ideas or time and effort to something
   - b.   to be one of the reasons that something happens
   - c.   something that you have written for a newspaper or magazine

5.   The new government <u>promotes</u> education and is planning to build new schools throughout the country.
   - a.   to support something to further its progress
   - b.   to advance someone to a preferable, more responsible job within an organization
   - c.   to encourage people to support or use something

6.   Many companies today are operating on extremely tight <u>margins</u>.
   - a.   the column of space at the side of a page
   - b.   the difference in the number of points between the winners and the losers of a sports event or competition
   - c.   the difference between what it costs to buy or produce something and its selling price

Task 3   Word classes

3.1   **Look at the sentences. Decide what word class would fill each gap. Write *v* (verb), *n* (noun), *adj* (adjective) or *adv* (adverb) in the brackets after each gap.**

1.   The university should _____ (_v_) more facilities for disabled students.

2.   The government's policy is to allow banks to _____ (___) independently, free of external controls.

3.   Many people feel less _____ (___) as a result of the sharp rise in crime.

4.   A high _____ (___) of babies born to mothers who were smokers have a less than average body weight at birth.

5. They see education as the first _____ (___) in the battle to improve public health in this region.

6. Interest based on the amount of money originally invested and the interest already earned is known as _____ (___) interest.

Task 4 | Word families

4.1 **Choose the correct form of the word in brackets to complete the sentences. In the case of verbs, pay attention to the ending required, e.g., ~s, ~ed, ~ing.**

1. The average daily food ___requirement___ for an adult is between 2,000 and 3,000 calories. (require)

2. The most recent _____ of the research suggests that human activities have had an influence on the global climate. (assess)

3. Contrary to popular _____, vigorous exercise is not necessarily good for your health. (perceive)

4. Focusing on research and development will have _____ for short-term profitability. (imply)

5. The rise of budget airlines in Europe has meant that cheap air travel is now _____ to almost everyone in the European Union. (access)

6. _____, companies need to invest money in the business in order to grow. (logic)

4.2 **Choose the correct form of the word in brackets to complete the sentences.**

1. It is often difficult to ___adjust___ to a change of career. Some people fail to make the ___adjustment___ and simply go back to their old job. (adjust)

2. The plan has been drawn up in _____ with our Far Eastern partners. We attempted to _____ them at all stages of the project. (consult)

3. Living standards in the area are _____ rapidly. The main reason for this _____ is the continuing armed conflict in the region. (decline)

4. The US government claims that the weapons their planes use are very _____. The number of civilian casualties on the ground would suggest that this _____ is more theoretical than real. (precise)

5. _____ in the exchange rate is a requirement for continued growth. A _____ currency will encourage investment. (stable)

4.3   **Complete the following sentences using either:**
- the word in brackets; or
- a prefix from the box + the correct form of the word in brackets

re~	in~	un~	mis~	over~	under~

1. The government is concerned that healthcare is being managed in an <u>uneconomical</u> way and losing vast sums of money. (economical)

2. Compared with the problems people in the Third World have with diseases, our worries are _____. (significant)

3. The patient received serious injuries in the accident, but her vital organs were _____. (affected)

4. Statistics can sometimes be _____ and lead to overgeneralized conclusions. (reliable)

5. Countries like Canada are planning to _____ almost 100 per cent of their waste. (cycle)

6. The receptionist's instructions were both complicated and _____, with the result that I was late for the meeting. (precise)

Task 5	Collocations

5.1   **Using your knowledge of collocation and paying particular attention to the underlined words, complete the gaps in these sentences.**

The word class you need is given in brackets at the end of each sentence. In the case of verbs, pay attention to the ending required, e.g., ~ed, ~ing, ~s.

1. _Recent_ <u>studies</u> show that women still earn less than men for doing the same job. (adjective)

2. Maria was delighted to _____ the <u>opportunity</u> to talk to someone who shared her interest in classical music. (verb)

3. There is little or no scientific _____ to <u>support</u> this <u>theory</u>. (noun)

4. Changes in energy policy will <u>have</u> a <u>huge</u> _____ on the environment. (noun)

5. The government is _____ the relief <u>effort</u> as numerous aid agencies arrive in the affected area. (verb)

6. The findings <u>confirmed</u> the _____ that smokers are at greater risk of heart attack. (noun)

7. The local economy <u>expanded</u> _____ during the 1980s and 1990s, but is currently in a period of crisis. (adverb)

Task 6 | Word grammar

6.1 **Look at the underlined nouns in the sentences below and identify:**

1. which nouns are followed by prepositions

2. which nouns are followed by *that* + clause

3. which nouns are followed by *to* + infinitive

a. There is clear <u>evidence</u> of a link between price reductions and increased sales. ___

b. The test measures children's <u>achievements</u> in different sports. ___

c. Cold Laser treatment is offered as an <u>alternative</u> to invasive surgery. ___

d. Many people take the <u>attitude</u> that mature students should be working rather than studying. ___

e. The government is concerned about its <u>capacity</u> to invest in the country's infrastructure. ___

6.2 **The verbs in the sentences below are sometimes transitive and sometimes intransitive. Look at the verbs as they are used in these sentences and decide if they are transitive (VT) or intransitive (VI).**

1. Teaching methods may <u>vary</u> depending on the target audience. ___

2. The research project will <u>focus</u> on the impact of e-business on an organization. ___

3. Gun owners had until the end of 1990 to <u>register</u> their weapons. ___

4. A lot of money has been <u>committed</u> to the reconstruction of the city. ___

5. My boss <u>declined</u> the offer. ___

Now check your answers in the key on page 202.

Appendix 3: Answer key

Unit 1: Multi-meaning words

Task 1

Ex 1.1

1.	c	7.	b
2.	a	8.	c
3.	b	9.	b
4.	a	10.	a
5.	a	11.	a
6.	b		

Ex 1.2

1.	a	6.	b
2.	b	7.	c
3.	b	8.	b
4.	b	9.	b
5.	a	10.	b

Task 2

Ex 2.1

1.	b	6.	a
2.	b	7.	b
3.	b	8.	a
4.	a	9.	a
5.	b	10.	b

Ex 2.2

Example definitions:

1. society (noun): *people living together in organized groups, with rules and traditions governing the way they behave towards one another*
2. subject (noun): *an idea, topic, problem or situation that you discuss in speech or writing*
3. heated (adjective): *impassioned or highly emotional. Full of angry and excited feelings.*
4. perform (verb): *to work or do something (well, badly)*
5. concern (noun): *a feeling of worry, especially about something such as a social problem, etc.*
6. far (adjective): *to a great degree*

Task 3

Ex 3.1

1. adjective, verb, noun
2. noun, verb, adjective
3. noun, adjective
4. noun, verb
5. noun, verb, adjective, adverb
6. noun, verb
7. noun, verb
8. noun, verb
9. noun, verb

Unit 2: Word classes – nouns, verbs, adjectives and adverbs

Task 1

Ex 1.1

Nouns	Verbs
study	ranks
tests	have slipped
Mathematics	average
classes	
contrast	

Adjectives	Adverbs
developed	particularly
American	
advanced	
large	

Task 2

Ex 2.1

Word	Word class
growth	*noun*
entire	*adjective*
basically	*adverb*
avoid	*verb*
existence	*noun*
discover	*verb*
regular	*adjective*
relatively	*adverb*
provide	*verb*
prevent	*verb*
highly	*adverb*
security	*noun*

Ex 2.2

1.	v	7.	adv
2.	adv	8.	v
3.	adj	9.	n
4.	n	10.	adv
5.	n	11.	adj
6.	v	12.	v

Ex 2.3

1. discovered		7. basically	
2. relatively		8. avoid	
3. entire		9. existence	
4. security		10. highly	
5. growth		11. regular	
6. prevent		12. provide	

Task 3
Ex 3.1

Word	Word class
excess	*noun, adjective*
stem	*noun, verb*
match	*noun, verb*
influence	*noun, verb*
lack	*noun, verb*
spare	*noun, verb, adjective*
joint	*noun, adjective*
risk	*noun, verb*
sample	*noun, verb, adjective*
rank	*noun, verb, adjective*

Ex 3.2

1. adj	6. adj
2. adj	7. v
3. n	8. v
4. v	9. n
5. v	10. n

Ex 3.3

Word	Word class
net	*noun, verb, adjective*
experience	*noun, verb*
rates	*noun, verb*
double	*noun, verb, adjective, adverb*
essential	*noun, adjective*
support	*noun, verb*
ideal	*noun, adjective*
border	*noun, verb*
prompt	*noun, verb, adjective*
blame	*noun, verb*

Ex 3.4

1. adj	6. v
2. v	7. adj
3. v	8. n
4. v	9. adv
5. adj	10. v

Task 4
Ex 4.1

1. a. adjective		c. noun	
b. verb		d. adverb	
2. a. n; v		c. n; adj	
b. n; v		d. n; v	

Ex 4.2

Knowledge of word class helps understanding of how to use <u>words</u> effectively. The best way to understand what word class a word <u>belongs</u> to is to read it in the context of a <u>sentence</u> or a paragraph. It is helpful to know that some words can belong to two or <u>more</u> word classes. For example, *prompt* can be a noun, a <u>verb</u> or an adjective, and *spare* can be a <u>noun</u>, a verb or an adjective.

Unit 3: Word families and word parts

Task 1
Ex 1.1

Verb	Noun: same form or different?
change	✔
restrict	*restriction*
employ	*employment*
cause	✔
offer	✔
depend	*dependence*
claim	✔
decrease	✔
respond	*response*
influence	✔
suggest	*suggestion*
aim	✔
argue	*argument*
risk	✔
waste	✔

Task 2
Ex 2.1

Nouns	Verbs
behaviour	activate
development	calculate
difference	realize
equality	
formation	

Adjectives	Adverbs
appropriate	gradually
economical	
social	

Ex 2.2

Nouns	Verbs
~ion	~ize
~ment	~ate
~ence	
~ity	

Adjectives	Adverbs
~al	~ly
~ate	

Task 3

Ex 3.1

Prefixes	Example words
mono~	*monotone, monorail*
bi~	*bipolar, biannual*
re~	*rearrange, reboot*
inter~	*interpersonal, international*
anti~	*anticlimax, anticlockwise*
geo~	*geopolitics, geophysics*
post~	*postmodern, postgraduate*
micro~	*microclimate, microorganism*
semi~	*semidetached, semifinal*
sub~	*substandard, subconscious*
thermo~	*thermometer*

Ex 3.2

1. re~
2. post~
3. semi~
4. thermo~
5. micro~
6. inter~
7. sub~
8. geo~
9. anti~
10. bi~
11. mono~

Task 4

Ex 4.1

1. uncertainty
2. unsatisfactory
3. inefficient
4. unlikely
5. disappearance
6. unprincipled
7. abnormal
8. irrelevant
9. illegal
10. immoral
11. unpublished

Task 5

Ex 5.1/5.2

1. long (*adj*) - **e.** length (*n*)
2. need (*v*) - **d.** necessary (*adj*)
3. obey (*v*) - **b.** obedience (*n*)
4. poor (*adj*) - **a.** poverty (*n*)
5. loan (*n*) - **c.** lend (*v*)
6. space (*n*) - **g.** spatial (*adj*)
7. describe (*v*) - **f.** description (*n*)

Task 6

Ex 6.1

Nouns	Verbs
competition	compete
decision	decide
permission, permit	permit
economy	economize
origin	originate
complication	complicate
absence	
certainty	

Adjectives	Adverbs
competitive	competitively
decisive	decisively
permissible	
economic, economical	economically
original	originally
complicated	
absent	
certain	certainly

Ex 6.2

1. competition
2. certainty
3. absence
4. economically
5. original
6. decision
7. permission
8. complications

Task 7

Ex 7.1

1. believe; belief
2. explained; explanation
3. different; differences
4. argument; argue
5. difficult; difficulty
6. develop; development

Task 8

Ex 8.1

1. <u>mem</u>ory, <u>mem</u>orial, re<u>mem</u>ber, com<u>mem</u>orate
2. <u>cent</u>enary, per<u>cent</u>age, <u>cent</u>ury
3. trans<u>port</u>, <u>port</u>able, im<u>port</u>, ex<u>port</u>
4. bi<u>ology</u>, psych<u>ology</u>, ge<u>ology</u>
5. <u>tele</u>vision, <u>tele</u>phone, <u>tele</u>scope
6. <u>vis</u>ual, <u>vis</u>ion, <u>vis</u>ible
7. pro<u>spect</u>, re<u>spect</u>, per<u>spect</u>ive, <u>spect</u>ator
8. <u>photo</u>graph, tele<u>photo</u>, <u>photo</u>synthesis

Ex 8.2

1. mem
2. photo
3. tele
4. port
5. pect
6. cent
7. vis
8. ology

Task 9

Ex 9.2

1. compete: *competition, competitive, competitor*
2. compare: *comparison, comparative, compared*
3. direct: *direction, director, directed, misdirect*
4. prepare: *preparation, prepared, unprepared*
5. depend: *dependence, depending, dependent, independent*

(Sentences depend on students.)

Unit 4: Collocations

Task 1

Ex 1.1

1. a. design
   b. introduce
   c. observe
   d. present
2. a. developmental
   b. ingenious
   c. young
   d. basic

Task 2

Ex 2.1

a. to put, to be, to come under, to have, to express, to take
b. on, about, over, for
c. *to* + infinitive

Ex 2.2

1. doubt
   have no doubts about
   express doubts over
   there are doubts about
2. pressure
   put pressure on
   there is pressure on
   come under pressure to
3. opportunity
   there is an opportunity for
   have the opportunity to
   take the opportunity to

Ex 2.3

1. to
2. for
3. are
4. put
5. on
6. is
7. have

Task 3

Ex 3.1

1. make, have, cause
2. do, mean, have, be in, run
3. make, put in, be
4. make, have, cause
5. make, see, have, be (is)
6. achieve, have, produce
7. be (is), give, establish
8. be (is), bridge, fill, see, leave, find
9. lower, achieve, conform to, set
10. give, cause, have, show, create, express, voice

Task 4

Ex 4.1

1. with
2. between
3. on
4. over/about
5. on
6. between
7. with

Task 5

Ex 5.1

1. main
2. sole
3. particular
4. growing
5. huge
6. recent
7. practical
8. human
9. growing, public
10. greater

Ex 5.2

1. slight, dramatic, significant
2. big, important, significant, major, serious, minor, slight, fundamental
3. large, short, regular, steady, constant, endless, limited
4. high, low, normal, strict, moral

Task 6

Ex 6.1

1. effectively
2. significantly
3. especially
4. clearly
5. gradually
6. particularly
7. increasingly
8. relatively
9. probably
10. rapidly
11. strongly
12. comparatively

a. effectively: manage(d) effectively
   significantly: significantly reduce
   clearly: clearly stated
   gradually: gradually decreases
   increasingly: becoming increasingly
   probably: (was) probably caused
   rapidly: spread rapidly
   strongly: strongly disagrees

b. especially: especially important
   particularly: particularly useful
   increasingly: increasingly difficult
   relatively: relatively recent
   comparatively: comparatively easy

Task 7
Ex 7.1
Possible answers:

1. *have* trouble
   have an effect
   manage resources
   see a connection
2. have trouble *with*
   have an impact *on*
   do business *with*
3. widening *gap*
   sole *purpose*
   growing *demand*
4. *reduce* significantly
   spread rapidly
   stated clearly
5. *increasingly* difficult
   especially important
   particularly useful

Unit 5: Word grammar

Task 1
Ex 1.1

1. years after the discovery
   migrants from Europe
   dangers of migration
   passage to North America
2. year's wages
3. farm labourer

Task 2
Ex 2.2

Nouns	*that* + clause
belief	✔
notion	✔
theory	✔
view	✔
idea	✔
fact	✔
suggestion	✔

Task 3
Ex 3.1

a.	1	g.	1
b.	2	h.	1
c.	2	i.	1
d.	1; 1	j.	1
e.	1	k.	1; 1
f.	4	l.	2; 1

Ex 3.2

a.	for	i.	of
d.	of; of	j.	on
e.	of	k.	on; of
g.	for	l.	of
h.	of		

Ex 3.3

1.	1	7.	3
2.	3	8.	3
3.	2	9.	3
4.	2	10.	1
5.	1	11.	2
6.	1	12.	3

Ex 3.4

1. to
5. of
6. of
10. of

Task 4
Ex 4.1
Example words:

1. figures, employees, spokesman, policy
2. leader, town, research, price
3. technology, system, game, age
4. weight, family, page, heart
5. insurance, car, policy, director, employee
6. government, father, mother, authority, unemployment
7. business, exchange, tax, success, failure

Task 5
Ex 5.1

a.	3	f.	1
b.	2	g.	1
c.	2	h.	3
d.	3	i.	2
e.	3	j.	1

Ex 5.2

a.	for
d.	for
e.	for
h.	to

Ex 5.3

All words are possible: necessary, difficult, possible, clear, likely

Ex 5.4

1. common, customary, useful
2. common, certain, customary, useful
3. certain
4. common, certain, customary, bound, useful

Task 7

Ex 7.1

1. transitive
2. intransitive
3. intransitive
4. transitive
5. transitive
6. transitive
7. transitive
8. transitive
9. transitive
10. transitive

Ex 7.2

Transitive: present, include, describe, lack, mention, suggest

Intransitive: appear, belong, interfere, remain, result, rise

Ex 7.3

1. to
2. with

Ex 7.4

1. VI
2. VI
3. VI
4. VI
5. VT
6. VT
7. VT
8. VT

Task 8

Ex 8.1

Verb	*that* + clause
decrease	
behave	
state	✔
consider	✔
admit	✔
introduce	

Ex 8.2

2. (was) agreed
3. suggests
4. (is worth) mentioning

5. claim
6. (have) discovered
8. (have come to) accept
9. admitted

Task 9

Ex 9.2

Verb	*wh~* word
doubt	*whether, what*
consider	*whether, what, which, when, why*
determine	*whether, what, which, when, why*
explain	*whether, what, when, why*
decide	*whether, what, which, when, why*
describe	*whether, what, which, when, why*
realize	*whether, what, which, when, why*
discuss	*whether, what, which, when, why*

Phrase completion: Answers depend on students.

Ex 9.3

1. The secretary will explain how you have to fill in the forms.
2. We need to discuss what kind of strategy we want for next year.
3. Many people doubt whether the new government will live up to the promises made in the election campaign.
4. The candidates are usually asked to describe why they would be suitable for the position.
5. The IT manager is considering whether the system currently in place should be updated.
6. People have a right to decide what they should do with their own money.

Task 10

Ex 10.1

Example words:

1. show, argue, suggest
2. explain, ask, discover
3. evidence, suggestion, answer
4. clear, possible, likely
5. customary, common, useful

Unit 6: AWL – Sublist 1

Task 1

Ex 1.2

1. <u>require</u> – **g.** to need something or someone
2. <u>vary</u> – **k.** to change or be different in different circumstances
3. <u>proceed</u> – **e.** to carry on doing something that has already started

4. <u>approach</u> – **f.** a way of dealing with a situation or problem

5. <u>evident</u> – **b.** easily seen or understood

6. <u>factor</u> – **h.** one of the things that causes a situation or influences the way it happens

7. <u>assume</u> – **a.** to accept something as true, although you do not have proof

8. <u>occur</u> – **l.** to happen

9. <u>available</u> – **d.** able to be found, bought or obtained

10. <u>interpret</u> – **c.** to take actions or behaviours as having a particular meaning

11. <u>derive</u> – **i.** to obtain or come from another source

12. <u>respond</u> – **j.** to say or do something in reaction to something else

Ex 1.3
1. derived; derive
2. occurs; occur
3. require; requires
4. evident; evident
5. approach; approaches
6. assumed; assume
7. varies; vary
8. interpreted; interpret
9. factors; factor
10. proceed; proceeding

Task 2
Ex 2.1

1.	a	7.	a
2.	b	8.	b
3.	c	9.	a
4.	b	10.	c
5.	c	11.	b
6.	b		

Task 3
Ex 3.1

Word	Word class
focus	*verb, noun*
benefit	*verb, noun*
research	*verb, noun*
policy	*noun*
individual	*noun, adjective*
function	*verb, noun*
assess	*verb*
specific	*noun, adjective*
finance	*verb, noun*
consist (of/in)	*verb*
identify	*verb*

Ex 3.2

1.	n	7.	adj
2.	v	8.	v
3.	adj	9.	n
4.	n	10.	v
5.	n	11.	v
6.	v		

Ex 3.3

1.	focus	7.	specific
2.	benefit	8.	identify
3.	individual	9.	finance
4.	research	10.	function
5.	policy	11.	consists
6.	assess		

Task 4
Ex 4.1

Nouns	Verbs
assessment	assess
economy	vary
variation	analyze
analysis	indicate
significance	respond
indication	create
response	interpret
environment	define
creation	
interpretation	
definition	

Adjectives	Adverbs
economic	economically
economical	significantly
variable	environmentally
significant	
indicative	
responsive	
creative	

Ex 4.2

1.	requirement	7.	analysis
2.	significant	8.	assessment
3.	variations	9.	indicate
4.	interpreted	10.	responded
5.	create	11.	environmental
6.	definition		

Ex 4.3

1. invariably
2. insignificant
3. unavailable
4. recreate
5. uneconomical
6. misinterpret
7. unresponsive
8. reassess
9. inconsistent
10. overestimate/underestimate

Ex 4.4

1. uneconomical
2. occur
3. unavailable
4. inconsistent
5. insignificant
6. responsive
7. misinterpreted
8. reassess
9. underestimated

Task 5

Ex 5.1

1. require - **f.** a special diet
2. interpret - **e.** data
3. meet - **d.** requirements
4. carry out **- b.** research
5. adopt - **g.** a policy
6. identify - **c.** the person
7. assess - **a.** effects

Ex 5.2

1. analyze
2. play
3. define
4. adopt
5. establish
6. estimate
7. assess
8. create

Ex 5.3

1. income
2. issues
3. methods
4. a theory
5. an analysis
6. benefit

Ex 5.4

1. shows
2. provides
3. obtain
4. show
5. collecting
6. support
7. needed
8. (has) shown
9. provide
10. examining
11. adopt
12. claim
13. (has) brought
14. used

Task 6

Ex 6.1

1. **b.** of
   d. about
   e. of
   f. for
   h. of
   i. of
   j. of
   k. to
   l. to
   m. in
   n. to
   o. from
   p. of
   q. of
   r. on
2. **a.** theory
   c. assumption
   g. evidence
3. **r.** questionnaire approach

Ex 6.2

1. government, makers, decisions
2. government, team, findings
3. analysis, collection
4. collection, decision-making, production

Ex 6.3

1. energy, light, power
2. costs, shortages, force, market, movement
3. social, housing, child, unemployment, concert
4. market, industry, licence, price
5. code, key, surface

Ex 6.4

Transitive verbs: assume, create, distribute, finance, involve, issue, process

Intransitive verbs: proceed, function, legislate, occur

Ex 6.5

Answers depend on students.

Ex 6.6

Answers depend on students.

Ex 6.7
1. VT
2. VI
3. VT
4. VI
5. VI
6. VT
7. VI

Ex 6.8
1. estimate – VT
2. require – VT
3. varies – VI
4. indicates – VT
5. define – VT
6. is proceeding – VI
7. has identified – VT
8. to establish – VT
9. include – VT
10. involving – VT

Task 7
Ex 7.1
Answers depend on students.

Ex 7.2
Answers depend on students.

Ex 7.3
Answers depend on students.

Unit 7: AWL – Sublist 2

Task 1
Ex 1.2
1. appropriate – h. right for a specific use
2. equate – j. to treat two things as equal or the same
3. affect – f. to change or influence someone or something
4. restrict – c. to ensure something stays within a limit or limits
5. distinct – i. obviously different or part of a contradictory type
6. potential – g. the possibilities that something or someone has to offer
7. feature – d. one of many parts of an idea or situation
8. complex – a. made up of multiple parts and often complicated
9. consequent – b. happening as a result of something
10. aspect – e. a part of something that stands out as being important or interesting

Ex 1.3
1. affected; affects
2. distinct; distinct
3. features; feature
4. complex; complex
5. potential; potentially
6. appropriate; appropriate

7. consequences; consequence
8. equate; equated
9. restrict; restricted
10. aspects; aspect

Task 2
Ex 2.1
1. c
2. b
3. a
4. c
5. a
6. a
7. a
8. c
9. c
10. a

Task 3
Ex 3.1
Word	Word class
conclude	verb
acquire	verb
community	noun
relevant	adjective
potential	noun, adjective
resource	verb, noun
transfer	verb, noun
focus	verb, noun
previous	adjective
secure	verb, adjective

Ex 3.2
1. v
2. v
3. adj
4. n
5. n
6. v
7. adj
8. adj
9. v
10. adj

Ex 3.3
1. focuses
2. concluded
3. potential
4. resources
5. community
6. transfer
7. relevant
8. secure
9. acquire
10. previous

Task 4

Ex 4.1

Nouns	Verbs	Adjectives
achievement	achieve	normal
normality	participate	strategic
participant	maintain	selective
participation	perceive	regional
maintenance	regulate	resourceful
perception	select	complex
regulation	computerize	distinct
strategy		
region		
resource		
complexity		
distinction		
computer		

Ex 4.2

1. perception
2. participation
3. achievements
4. strategy
5. distinction
6. consequence
7. maintenance
8. assistance
9. selective
10. regulations

Ex 4.3

1. insecure
2. irrelevant
3. unregulated
4. inappropriate
5. reconstruct
6. unaffected
7. abnormal
8. reinvest
9. unobtainable
10. unrestricted
11. inconclusive

Ex 4.4

1. inappropriate
2. irrelevant
3. unrestricted
4. abnormal
5. unaffected
6. construction
7. regulated
8. reinvest
9. unobtainable
10. inconclusive

Task 5

Ex 5.1

1. <u>exploit</u> – **c.** the potential of something
2. <u>make</u> – **d.** a distinction
3. <u>affect</u> – **f.** one's health
4. <u>attract</u> – **a.** investment
5. <u>conduct</u> – **b.** an investigation
6. <u>restrict</u> – **e.** access

Ex 5.2

1. achieve
2. affect
3. maintain
4. perceive
5. consume
6. design
7. transfer
8. evaluate

Ex 5.3

1. complex
2. primary
3. positive
4. final
5. normal
6. appropriate

Ex 5.4

a. *to reduce (the), to have (an) increased, enforce make (a) to lift; to impose to have; to face (the) to commission (a)* — *impact regulations distinction restrictions consequences report*

b. *aspect(s) of participation in relevant (to) regulation of range of* — *life; the problem the research; elections information, to our work the Internet and media products; solutions*

c. *vast; wide huge environmental and ecological far-reaching* — *range impact aspect(s) consequences*

d. *particularly* — *relevant*

Task 6

Ex 6.1

1. a. between
   b. of
   c. of
   e. of
   f. on; of
   g. in
   h. of
   i. in
   j. by
   k. on; of
   l. of
   m. for
   n. of

2. d. perception

Ex 6.2

1. consumption
2. computer
3. construction
4. restrictions

Ex 6.3

1. marketing; corporate; business; development; strategy
2. work; planning; building; health; safety
3. state; job; guard; light; risk; service; forces; procedures; firm
4. accounts; course; college

Ex 6.4

Transitive verbs: categorize, equate, evaluate, design, injure, purchase, seek, credit, feature, finalize, regulate, secure, perceive, select, survey

Intransitive verbs: participate, reside

Ex 6.5

Answers depend on students.

Ex 6.6

Answers depend on students.

Ex 6.7

1. VT	**4.** VI
2. VI	**5.** VT
3. VI	**6.** VI

Task 7

Ex 7.1

Possible answers:

1. distinct parts
   complex relationship
   primary objective
   vast range
   relevant information
2. feature writers
   exercise routines
   children's achievements
   voter participation
   exchange restrictions
3. credit for
   aspects of
   distinction between
   consequences of
   impact on
4. focus
   transfer
   resource
   conduct
   design

Ex 7.2

Answers depend on students.

Ex 7.3

Answers depend on students.

Unit 8: AWL – Sublist 3

Task 1

Ex 1.2

1. <u>component</u> – **f.** one of the many parts that make up a machine or system
2. <u>excluding</u> – **i.** not including
3. <u>initial</u> – **d.** happening when something first starts
4. <u>constrain</u> – **h.** to prevent or limit something
5. <u>consent</u> – **c.** to allow something to happen
6. <u>deduce</u> – **a.** to produce an opinion as a result of information

7. <u>dominant</u> – **b.** stronger or more obvious than other people or things which are similar
8. <u>core</u> – **e.** the strongest members of a group
9. <u>layer</u> – **j.** one of several levels within an organization
10. <u>outcome</u> – **g.** the results or consequences of something

Ex 1.3

1. component; components	**6.** deduce; deduced
2. dominated; dominant	**7.** layer; layers
3. initial; initially	**8.** core; cores
4. constrained; constrain	**9.** outcome; outcomes
5. excluding; excludes/excluded	**10.** consent; consented

Task 2

Ex 2.1

1. c	**8.** a
2. b	**9.** a
3. a	**10.** a
4. c	**11.** b
5. b	**12.** b
6. c	**13.** a
7. b	**14.** b

Task 3

Ex 3.1

Word	Word class
shift	*noun, verb*
link	*noun, verb*
proportion	*noun*
sequence	*noun, verb*
volume	*noun*
alternative	*noun, adjective*
consent	*noun, verb*
minority	*noun*
register	*noun, verb*
specify	*verb*
comment	*noun, verb*
emphasize	*verb*

Ex 3.2

1. n	**7.** n
2. n	**8.** v
3. v	**9.** v
4. v	**10.** n
5. n	**11.** v
6. adj	**12.** v

Ex 3.3

1. volume
2. sequence
3. linked
4. emphasizes
5. proportion
6. alternative
7. consent
8. comment
9. specify
10. minorities
11. registered
12. shifting

Task 4

Ex 4.1

Nouns	Verbs
reaction	react
validation	specify
validity	rely
reliability	illustrate
reliance	locate
illustration	justify
location	imply
justification	correspond
implication	compensate
compensation	contribute
contribution	constrain
constraint	deduce
deduction	emphasize
proportion	
emphasis	

Adjectives	Adverbs
specific	initially
reliable	correspondingly
initial	alternatively
alternative	constantly
constant	exclusively
exclusive	sufficiently
proportional	
sufficient	

Ex 4.2

1. compensation
2. emphasis
3. initially
4. reaction
5. implications
6. specific
7. sufficiently
8. constantly
9. alternatively
10. contributions

Ex 4.3

1. invalidate
2. insufficient
3. unspecified
4. unreliable
5. disproportionate
6. relocate/dislocate
7. unjustified
8. unconventional

Ex 4.4

1. unreliable
2. invalidated
3. insufficient
4. relocate
5. unjustified

Task 5

Ex 5.1

1. meet
2. demonstrate
3. make
4. justify
5. pay
6. follow
7. coordinating
8. given
9. predict
10. has been
11. maximize

Ex 5.2

1. justify
2. illustrate
3. shift
4. dominate
5. emphasize
6. exclude

Ex 5.3

1. Children; excluded
2. illustrate; point
3. emphasizes; importance
4. dominate; world
5. shift; attention

Ex 5.4

1. <u>initial</u> – **f.** performance
2. <u>ethnic</u> – **e.** minorities
3. <u>positive</u> – **g.** outcome
4. <u>dominant</u> – **a.** male
5. <u>particular</u> – **c.** treatment
6. <u>different</u> – **h.** components
7. <u>alternative</u> – **j.** techniques
8. <u>valid</u> – **b.** reasons
9. <u>enormous</u> – **i.** shift
10. <u>full</u> – **d.** compensation

Ex 5.5

Possible answers:

1. reaction; impression
2. evidence; food; money; means
3. point; place; person; group; detail; thing
4. ticket; document; agreement; reason; argument; criticism
5. person; friend; worker; source; type
6. offence; illness; injury; change; importance; issue

Ex 5.6

a.
draw up; provide	a framework
have	implications
draw up	criteria
make	a contribution

b.
serious; social; environmental	implications
certain; exceptional	circumstances
only; new	criterion/criteria
significant; small	proportion
first	reaction
prior; written	consent
huge; significant	contribution

c.
criterion/criteria	*for*
framework	*with; for*
proportion	*of*
reaction	*to*

d.
under; in	circumstances
with	consent

Task 6

Ex 6.1

1.
a.	to	i.	of
d.	for	j.	of
e.	of	k.	for
f.	on	l.	to
g.	of	m.	to
h.	of	n.	of

2. c. implication
3. h. *at (the)* core
   i. *across (many)* instances
4. l. schemes
5. b. alternative

Ex 6.2

1. <u>construction</u> – **b.** project
2. <u>ozone</u> – **c.** layer
3. <u>climate</u> – **a.** change
4. <u>repair</u> – **f.** work
5. <u>car</u> – **i.** engine
6. <u>shellfish</u> – **d.** fossils
7. <u>flood</u> – **j.** defenses
8. <u>stock</u> – **h.** exchange
9. <u>peer</u> – **e.** pressure
10. <u>transport</u> – **g.** infrastructure

Ex 6.3

Transitive verbs: fund, negate, publish, remove, specify, deduce, imply, ensure
Intransitive verbs: consent, correspond, interact

Ex 6.4
Answers depend on students.

Ex 6.5
Answers depend on students.

Ex 6.6
1. VT		4. VT	
2. VI		5. VT	
3. VI			

Ex 6.7
Answers depend on students.

Ex 6.8
1. The two stories illustrate why we need better and cheaper health care.
2. Good tests allow students to demonstrate what they can do.
3. The contract specifies when the machines have to be delivered.
4. Regulations specify how many hours drivers can work.
5. The prime minister emphasized what we need to do to rebuild the economy.
6. The contract clearly specifies who is not covered by the agreement.
7. The rumours about her pregnancy illustrate why you should not always believe tabloid newspapers.

Task 7

Ex 7.1

Possible answers:

1. initial performance
   positive outcome
   core audience
   ethnic minorities
   active contribution
2. aid agencies
   ozone layer
   football management
   government scheme
   stock exchange
3. outcome
   contribution
   shift
   proportion
   alternative
4. consent
   fund
   shift
   scheme
   link

Ex 7.2

Answers depend on students.

Ex 7.3

Answers depend on students.

Unit 9: AWL – Sublist 4

Task 1

Ex 1.2

1. integrate – **e.** when two or more suitable things are connected to work together more effectively than before
2. implement – **h.** to make something happen that has been officially decided
3. subsequent – **j.** following on from or coming after something else
4. overall – **f.** including everything or considering something as a whole
5. attribute – **g.** to believe that a situation or event is caused by something
6. apparent – **a.** obvious or easy to notice
7. hence – **c.** for this reason or as a result of this
8. impose – **b.** to force people to accept something
9. adequate – **d.** good enough or sufficient for a specific purpose
10. prior – **i.** happening previous to a particular time

Ex 1.3

1. subsequent	6. adequate; adequately
2. attributed	7. prior
3. impose; imposed	8. apparently; apparent
4. hence	9. integrate; integrated
5. overall	10. implement; implemented

Task 2

Ex 2.1

1. c	6. a
2. a	7. a
3. b	8. a
4. a	9. a
5. b	10. b

Task 3

Ex 3.1

Word	Word class
stress	*verb, noun*
grant	*verb, noun*
hypothesis	*noun*
civil	*adjective*
contrast	*verb, noun*
cycle	*verb, noun*
internal	*adjective*
resolve	*verb, noun*
principal	*noun, adjective*
access	*verb, noun*
label	*verb, noun*
phase	*verb, noun*

Ex 3.2

1. n	7. v
2. n	8. v
3. adj	9. v
4. n	10. v
5. v	11. adj
6. n	12. adj

Ex 3.3

1. cycle	7. contrast
2. hypothesis	8. resolve
3. principal	9. labelled
4. access	10. granted
5. stressed	11. internal
6. phase	12. civil

Task 4

Ex 4.1

Nouns	Verbs
concentration	concentrate
promotion	promote
debate	predict
statistics	investigate
investigation	occupy
occupation	
option	
access	

Adjectives	Adverbs
annual	annually
debatable	predictably
predictable	statistically
occupational	apparently
optional	
apparent	
accessible	

Ex 4.2

1. investigation
2. statistics
3. predictable
4. accessible
5. concentrations
6. occupations
7. promotion
8. option
9. debatable
10. predictably
11. Apparently

Ex 4.3

1. investigating; investigations
2. debated; debate
3. access; accessible
4. occupied; occupation
5. predict; predictions
6. investigation; investigators
7. communication; communicators

Ex 4.4

1. inaccessible
2. inadequate
3. uncommunicative
4. recycle
5. unresolved
6. unpredictable

Ex 4.5

1. inadequate
2. recycle
3. accessible
4. unpredictable
5. unresolved
6. uncommunicative

Task 5

Ex 5.1

1. occupy France
2. grant permission
3. implement a strategy
4. impose a ban/limits/a fine
5. give access/recommendations/permission
6. stress the need
7. carry out an investigation
8. have no option
9. investigate the causes

Ex 5.2

1. promote
2. predict
3. retain
4. commit
5. stress
6. undertake

Ex 5.3

1. promotes; growth
2. retain; control
3. stress; importance
4. undertook; task
5. commit; crimes
6. predicting; growth

Ex 5.4

1. subsequent – f. waiting times
2. prior – a. notice
3. emotional – d. problems
4. inadequate – b. provision
5. overall – e. strategy
6. chief – c. concern

Ex 5.5

Possible answers:

1. analysis, method, technique
2. market, trend, democracy
3. impression, cost, majority
4. policy, wall, measurements, injury, inquiry, mail, trade, security
5. provisions, amount, funding, job
6. market, flight, appliance, life, violence
7. agreement, arrangement, engagement, warning, notice
8. defence, servant, law, liberty, order, authority, disobedience, engineering
9. case, question, situation
10. cause, issue, source, character

Ex 5.6

a. place (stress)
b. need (access)
c. confirm (hypothesis)
d. (statistics) show
e. make (predictions)
f. require (concentration)
g. commit (error)
h. break (cycle)
i. have (status)
j. have (options)
k. achieve (goals)

Ex 5.7

a.
official	statistics
experimental	phase
high	concentration
emotional	stress
economic; latest	predictions
high social	status
definite	goals

b.
According to	statistics
of	stress
in	phase

c.
integrated	*fully*
promoted	*aggressively*
accessible	*easily*
communicate	*effectively*
contrasts	*sharply*

Task 6

Ex 6.1

1. a. to
    b. towards
    d. in
    e. of
    f. for
    k. of
    l. about
    m. to
    n. to
    o. between
    p. to
    q. of
2. c. attitude
    r. hypothesis
3. l. debate
4. d. in
5. a. job
    m. commitment
6. h. despite, preposition, noun (the fact)
    i. Despite, preposition, noun (their hard work)

Ex 6.2

1. <u>energy</u> – **f.** policy
2. <u>life</u> – **e.** expectancy
3. <u>distribution</u> – **d.** costs
4. <u>prison</u> – **b.** sentence
5. <u>weather</u> – **a.** conditions
6. <u>research</u> – **g.** project
7. <u>military</u> – **c.** regime

Ex 6.3

Possible answers:

1. area, security, computer, bar, name
2. human, computer, spelling
3. management, school
4. defence, survival, escape

Ex 6.4

a. 3. evident
    5. significant
    9. appropriate
    11. positive
    15. obvious
    16. predictable
b. 4. illegal
    8. appropriate
    10. abnormal
c. 1. available
    2. economical
    6. sufficient
    12. traditional
    13. valid
d. use of *whether*

Ex 6.5

1. active
2. passive
3. active
4. passive
5. active

Ex 6.6

Transitive verbs: access, domesticate, implicate, internalize,
Intransitive verbs: emerge

Ex 6.7

Answers depend on students.

Ex 6.8

Answers depend on students.

Ex 6.9

1. VI
2. VT
3. VT
4. VI
5. VT
6. VI
7. VI
8. VT
9. VT
10. VI
11. VT
12. VI

Ex 6.10

Answers depend on students.

Ex 6.11

Answers depend on students.

Task 7

Ex 7.1

Possible answers:

1. prior notice
    new policies
    difficult childhood
    criminal code
    modern world
2. trade union
    job security
    customer service
    school leavers
    university counsellor
3. stress
    investigation
    contrast
    commitment
    error
4. stress
    cycle
    contrast
    debate
    resolve

Ex 7.2

Answers depend on students.

Ex 7.3

Answers depend on students.

Unit 10: AWL – Sublist 5

Task 1

Ex 1.2

1. <u>aware</u> – **f.** to know of something's existence
2. <u>challenge</u> – **h.** something which tests a person's energy and determination
3. <u>enforce</u> – **d.** to ensure someone abides by something
4. <u>substitute</u> – **e.** something that is used instead of the thing that you normally use, because the usual thing is not available
5. <u>fundamental</u> – **n.** the most essential and simple part of something
6. <u>trend</u> – **k.** a subtle change or development that seems likely to continue
7. <u>symbol</u> – **a.** a person or thing that is thought of as representing a bigger idea
8. <u>welfare</u> – **g.** the health and happiness of a person
9. <u>revenue</u> – **j.** the monetary gain that a business organization receives, often from sales
10. <u>modify</u> – **l.** to make small changes to something to increase its effectiveness
11. <u>facilitate</u> – **c.** to allow something to happen in an easier way
12. <u>stability</u> – **b.** the state of staying balanced and not altering
13. <u>transition</u> – **i.** the change from one form or state to another
14. <u>ratio</u> – **m.** how two things relate to each other as numbers

Ex 1.3

1. fundamental; fundamentally
2. revenue; revenue
3. aware; aware
4. substitute; substituted
5. stable; stable
6. welfare; welfare
7. challenge; challenging
8. trends; trend
9. enforces; enforced
10. modified; modify
11. facilitated; facilitate

12. symbols; symbolic
13. transition; transition
14. ratio; ratio

Task 2

Ex 2.1

1. a		7. a	
2. c		8. b	
3. b		9. a	
4. b		10. a	
5. a		11. a	
6. b		12. b	

Task 3

Ex 3.1

Word	Word class
prime	*noun, verb, adjective*
conflict	*noun, verb*
decline	*noun, verb*
challenge	*noun, verb*
contact	*noun, verb*
compound	*noun, verb, adjective*
monitor	*noun, verb*
network	*noun, verb*
reject	*noun, verb*
objective	*noun, adjective*
target	*noun, verb*
alternate	*verb, adjective*

Ex 3.2

1. n		7. v	
2. n		8. n	
3. v		9. n	
4. adj		10. adj	
5. adj		11. adj	
6. n		12. v	

Ex 3.3

1. decline		7. rejected	
2. contact		8. network	
3. monitors		9. challenge	
4. prime		10. compound	
5. alternate		11. objective	
6. conflict		12. target	

Task 4

Ex 4.1

Nouns	Verbs
modification	modify
symbol	sustain
substitution	substitute
rejection	reject
precision	evolve
evolution	consult
logic	expand
consultation	adjust
expansion	
adjustment	

Adjectives	Adverbs
symbolic	precisely
sustainable	logically
stable	

Ex 4.2

1. alter
2. expansion
3. adjustment
4. evolved
5. Precision
6. Logically
7. stability
8. symbolic
9. substitution
10. rejection
11. sustain
12. modifications

Ex 4.3

1. expand; expansion
2. adjust; adjustment
3. stability; stable
4. evolve; evolution
5. aware; awareness
6. consultation; consult
7. declining; decline
8. precise; precision

Ex 4.4

1. readjustment
2. unaware
3. redraft
4. illogical
5. unsustainable
6. unmonitored
7. imprecise
8. instability

Ex 4.5

1. illogical
2. aware
3. redraft
4. monitored
5. unsustainable
6. stability
7. imprecise

Task 5

Ex 5.1

1. enforce – **f.** laws
2. reduce – **d.** taxes
3. show – **b.** signs
4. make – **c.** the transition
5. face – **e.** a challenge
6. threaten – **i.** stability
7. safeguard – **a.** welfare
8. facilitate – **j.** work flow
9. exceed – **h.** input
10. raise – **g.** awareness

Ex 5.2

1. draft
2. challenge
3. sustain
4. monitor
5. generate
6. reject
7. pursue
8. alter

Ex 5.3

1. draft; constitution
2. rejected; proposal
3. generated; jobs
4. monitor; progress
5. challenge; decision
6. pursue; interests
7. sustain; economic
8. alter; fact

Ex 5.4

1. fundamental – **g.** tasks
2. present – **e.** staff
3. lost – **d.** revenue
4. different – **i.** versions
5. managerial – **a.** trends
6. prime – **c.** cause
7. principal – **h.** symbol
8. greater – **b.** awareness
9. rapid economic – **f.** expansion

Ex 5.5

Possible answers:

1. achievement, subject, standards, qualifications
2. diet, country, marriage, building
3. affair, pressure, wall, examiner, use, source
4. issue, point, change, difference, error
5. example, candidate, time, minister, factor, cost, target
6. conclusion, deduction, mind
7. analysis, fact, judgement
8. detail, cost, moment, nature, location

Ex 5.6

a.	an adjustment	make
	transition	make (the)
	capacity	work at; have (the)
	image	improve

conflict (with)	come into
modifications	make
its target	reach
b. adjustment	slight
(at) ~ capacity	reduced
perspective	historical; new
version	official
modifications	minor
c. evolving	rapidly
aware	increasingly
expanded	rapidly
monitoring	closely

Task 6

Ex 6.1

1.	**b.** of	**k.** of
	d. of	**m.** for
	e. of	**n.** to
	f. of	**o.** of
	g. from	**p.** about
	h. with	**q.** of
	i. of	**r.** in
	j. in	**s.** of

2. **c.** notion
3. **t.** trend
4. **h.** in consultation
   m. on target
5. **a.** capacity

Ex 6.2

1. of	5. of
2. of	6. to
3. of	7. on
4. of	

Ex 6.3

1. air – **f.** travel
2. work – **d.** flow
3. aviation – **a.** fuel
4. exchange – **g.** rate
5. transport – **b.** needs
6. passenger – **e.** safety
7. freedom – **j.** fighter
8. Internet – **h.** access
9. sales – **c.** target
10. interest – **i.** rates

Ex 6.4

Possible answers:

1. sales, production, date, level, audience
2. sugar, teacher
3. level
4. media, television, radio, computer, train
5. book, vote

Ex 6.5

a.	5. logical		
b.	2. aware		
	7. logical		
c.	1. to	6. about
	3. of	8. of
	4. to	

Ex 6.6

Transitive verbs: amend, contact, compound, expose, liberalize, enable, license, symbolize
Intransitive verbs: conflict

Ex 6.7

Answers depend on students.

Ex 6.8

Answers depend on students.

Ex 6.9

1. VT	8. VT
2. VI	9. VT
3. VT	10. VI
4. VT	11. VT
5. VT	12. VI
6. VI	13. VT
7. VI	14. VI

Task 7

Ex 7.1

Possible answers:

1. present trends
   local journalists
   prime cause
   official version
   rapid expansion
2. exchange-rate stability
   tax revenue
   fossil fuel substitutes
   temperature monitor
   sales targets
3. consultation
   adjustment
   capacity
   symbol
   transition
4. compound
   decline
   challenge
   source
   monitor

Ex 7.2

Answers depend on students.

Ex 7.3

Answers depend on students.

Task 1

Ex 1.1

1. available; available
2. varies; vary
3. restrict; restricted
4. dominant; dominant
5. apparent; apparent
6. aware; aware

Task 2

Ex 2.1

1. a
2. c
3. a
4. b
5. a
6. c

Task 3

Ex 3.1

1. v
2. v
3. adj
4. n
5. n
6. adj

Task 4

Ex 4.1

1. requirement
2. assessment
3. perception
4. implications
5. accessible
6. Logically

Ex 4.2

1. adjust; adjustment
2. consultation; consult
3. declining; decline
4. precise; precision
5. Stability; stable

Ex 4.3

1. uneconomical
2. insignificant
3. unaffected
4. unreliable
5. recycle
6. imprecise

Task 5

Ex 5.1

1. Recent
2. have
3. evidence
4. impact/effect
5. coordinating/monitoring
6. hypothesis/theory
7. rapidly

Task 6

Ex 6.1

a. 1
b. 1
c. 1
d. 2
e. 3

Ex 6.2

1. VI
2. VI
3. VT
4. VT
5. VT